Random Illuminations

Also by ELEANOR WACHTEL

Original Minds
More Writers & Company
Writers & Company
Language in Her Eye (edited, with Libby Scheier and Sarah Sheard)
The Expo Story (edited, with Robert Anderson)

Conversations with **Carol Shields**

Random Illuminations

ELEANOR WACHTEL

Cover photograph by Neil Graham.
Cover design by Kent Fackenthall and Julie Scriver.
Book design by Julie Scriver.
Printed in Canada.
10 9 8 7 6 5 4 3 2 1

Library and Archives Canada Cataloguing in Publication

Wachtel, Eleanor
Random illuminations: conversations with Carol Shields / Eleanor Wachtel.

ISBN 978-0-86492-501-5 (pbk.)

1. Shields, Carol, 1935-2003 — Interviews.
2. Shields, Carol, 1935-2003 — Correspondence.
3. Wachtel, Eleanor — Correspondence.
4. Authors, Canadian (English) — 20th century — Interviews. I. Title.
PS8587.H46Z54 2007   C813'.54   C2007-904305-4

Goose Lane Editions acknowledges the financial support of the Canada Council for the Arts, the Government of Canada through the Book Publishing Industry Development Program (BPIDP), and the New Brunswick Department of Wellness, Culture and Sport for its publishing activities.

Goose Lane Editions
Suite 330, 500 Beaverbrook Court
Fredericton, New Brunswick
CANADA E3B 5X4
www.gooselane.com

for SLS

&

for Don

and Sara, Catherine, Meg,
Anne, and John

Contents

Preface

Not long ago, I was sitting in a restaurant on the Bosphorus in Istanbul with some Turkish academics discussing a new translation of a novel by their Nobel Prize winner, Orhan Pamuk. Somehow in the conversation, Carol Shields's name was mentioned. How wonderful a writer she is, said one; how fine her sense of language, said another. "I've read all her books except *The Box Garden*," she continued. "I wanted to save one, to know it was there waiting for me." For a moment I wondered if they realized she was no longer alive; they were speaking in the present. Their excitement made me long to tell Carol about them, how pleased and amused she would be by their enthusiasm — halfway around the world. A few of her stories had been translated into Turkish but they were reading her in English — and loving it. Had I seen, they asked, that *Unless* is on a list of 1001 books to read before you die? I'd never heard of that, though we'd been joking about Istanbul's Turkish baths, which are famously on that *other* list of 1000 things to *do* before you die. But they were surprised when I told them I knew Carol, that she had been a friend, and yes, they knew sadly that she was dead.

This encounter highlighted what I want to do with this book: to honour Carol's memory and to celebrate how alive her voice is in today's world. To find her so present and so beloved in a faraway place like Turkey just brings to the fore the pain of her absence and simultaneously the delight of knowing that she still speaks to people everywhere.

I first interviewed Carol twenty years ago, when she published *Swann: A Mystery*. Soon after, I interviewed her again, at length, for a special issue of the feminist literary magazine *Room of One's Own* and for a profile I was writing for *Books in Canada*. Subsequently, I interviewed her with every new book, occasionally on stage, five times in the last six years of her life. She was thoughtful, open and always engaged. As I say elsewhere, I loved how her mind worked — her curiosity, astuteness and compassion. These conversations offer richly faceted glimpses of Carol's world.

I have also included some of her correspondence, more or less chronologically between these interviews, letters she wrote me over the years, offering a slightly different angle of observation, often about the books she was reading and writing.

Random Illuminations begins with a personal essay, my own attempt to come to terms with her loss. And it ends with her reflections on death. But Carol was so attuned to the shape, to the arc of a human life, that it would be a disservice to frame hers elegiacally. In this first piece, a Scrapbook — kaleidoscopic, insistently unfinished — I also try to describe how she enriched my life and the lives of so many others. In the conversations that follow, she traces her childhood, including precocious sonnet writing, early marriage and motherhood, fledgling socialism and feminism, and the beginnings of her career as a poet, academic and novelist. She talks about how she approached her different books, in some cases their gestation as short stories, her ambitions, and the satisfactions and demands of her themes and characters. She discusses the significance of finding a "home" and the importance to her of conversation itself. As life deals her unexpected cards, she responds with characteristic generosity, courage, and depth. Therein lies abundance and joy.

April 2007

Scrapbook of Carol

It all started with the death of my mother, though unlike those yet to come, this first one was surprising, sudden and relatively quick. Strange, I suppose, to describe the death of an eighty-nine-year-old woman as surprising, but she was in good health, with a quick wit and only gradual loss of memory.

Born in Montreal in 1911 she was the first of her family to be born in Canada; her early life seemed to belong more to the nineteenth century than the twenty-first century in which she died. For instance, she never went to high school. Until Jean Lesage and the Quiet Revolution (until, in fact, *I* entered high school some thirty-eight years later in 1961), there were fees to attend public secondary school in Quebec. At the end of the first week of classes, the teacher came around to collect, and that was the end of my mother's formal education. She got work in a ladies' hat factory where her older sister already had a job, and from the age of twelve until she gave birth to my older brother almost twenty years later, she remained at the factory, at some point promoted to making samples. She held on to her job right through the Depression. Years later, she recalled packing lunches for her sister and herself — her most memorable was fresh tomato and lettuce on white bread. She could still taste it. I tried to imagine her in her early teens trundling off to work bearing sandwiches, but I could never get further than the factory entrance; in my mind, it always turned into a school.

First my mother, then four close friends died. The dedication page of the book of interviews I published the next year looked like a casualty list.

When I say it all started, I mean this particular period of my life, of loss. My very first encounter with death had been almost twenty years earlier when my father died. It was then that I learned how death renders life meaningless, how hard it is to recover any sense of meaning afterwards. He would come to me in dreams and I would be so excited to find him alive. When I awoke, I would try to mitigate the anguish of reality with some interpretation, an idea of communication, blessing, anything. After a while, he stopped coming. But I couldn't escape the memory of how wretched he was those last two weeks of his life, how he didn't go gentle, not at all. What I learned was that certain kinds of loss are irrecoverable; while the acuteness may dull, the hollow is never filled. But I'd had two decades to forget that lesson.

"Grief turns out to be a place none of us knows until we reach it," writes Joan Didion in *The Year of Magical Thinking*. "Nor can we know ahead of the fact (and here lies the heart of the difference between grief as we imagine it and grief as it is) the unending absence that follows, the void, the very opposite of meaning, the relentless succession of moments during which we will confront the experience of meaninglessness itself." I read those words just when I started to think again about all these deaths, when T.S. Eliot's epigraph to *The Waste Land* (from Dante's *Inferno*) kept reverberating in my head: "I had not thought death had undone so many."

My mother's death was used by a journalist from the *Globe and Mail* as the occasion to introduce the subject of mothers and death in her profile about Carol Shields. My mother died in Toronto on the night of the opening of the musical version of *Larry's Party*. Carol was in town for the premiere; I had been scheduled to attend but instead we met for lunch the next day. When I walked Carol back to her hotel, the journalist was waiting to interview her.

Carol's diagnosis was the first and her death the last of that awful time, but that made it no easier to accept. If anything, I had become accustomed to the idea that she was ill, very ill at times, but surely, I thought, she would go on and on this way. She was always such good company, terrific to talk to — even at chemo sessions. Or after an hour-long telephone conversation, I'd remark on how good she sounded. Sometimes, she'd then admit she actually wasn't, but it was her engagement with the world that sustained her; she was able to keep that curiosity and interest for an amazingly long time.

Every now and then, Carol and I would go to the movies. Five months before she died, we went to see *The Hours*, which was based on a novel that neither of us liked very much. But she enjoyed the film, especially because it gave her images she could conjure up later and reflect on. There was a line in the film about staying alive for the people you love, and I asked if she thought that was true. She said no, you stay alive for yourself, but you might endure some extra medical treatment for the people you love. And I remembered her having recently asked me about whether she should have more treatment. And how I knew I was giving her the wrong answer when I said yes. But I wanted more. (I still do.)

Back then, she reassured me that "sixty-seven is a ripe old age. I was supposed to have twenty-two months; I've had more than double that. I wrote a book, two books," she continued. "I'd love to write the sonnet novel but don't seem to have the energy." At this point she was taking Tylenol 3 but never complained of pain. She wrote letters to all her children and grandchildren, and several to her husband. "I made a New Year's resolution," she said, "not to worry about the kids. I want them to have everything." (This final novel project, set in her hometown near Chicago and about a woman in her sixties who writes sonnets, remained unfinished when she died. Called "Segue," an excerpt was featured in the posthumously published *Collected Stories*.)

Our talk might start with books but the conversations, hundreds of them over the years, would go everywhere — from napkin etiquette and models for dying to an unexpurgated version of dinner with the Queen and Prince Philip.

When I look back now, to her letters, our conversations, her

books, I divide it all into Before and After. Before the diagnosis and
during her illness.

I first met Carol in 1980 at the Literary Storefront in Vancouver's
Gastown. I'd already reviewed *The Box Garden* for the *Vancouver
Sun* and subsequently reviewed her other novels, but I didn't really
get to know her until she published *Swann: A Mystery* in the fall of
1987. By this time she was living in Winnipeg and I'd just moved to
Toronto as the "literary commentator" for CBC Radio's *State of the
Arts*. I did a radio piece about the novel and liked the book so much
that I decided to put together a special double issue on Carol for the
journal *Room of One's Own*. That was the first time I interviewed
her. What a luxury it was: it took place over two days. She came to
my flat, and I took a few photographs to include in the magazine
along with an assortment she chose from her early family life. The
next time, we met for lunch. I used this as a scene setter when I wrote
a cover story about Carol for *Books in Canada*.

> Carol Shields is sitting at a restaurant, looking like a character
> from one of her early novels. What used to be called sensibly
> dressed: a soft cream-coloured sweater fastened at the neck
> with a gold bow pin. Matching skirt, pumps. Simple stud ear-
> rings; pearl ring and gold bracelet on one hand; gold wedding
> band and diamond engagement ring on the other. Shields is
> thin, with short blonde hair and clear blue eyes behind thick-
> lensed glasses, which she removes and folds on the table. She
> has a small, soft, sometimes hesitant voice. She admits to a cer-
> tain passivity, a reticence. And then disarms by saying, "Okay,
> ask me something personal."

I remember a lot of those first conversations — for instance, how
Carol's learning to read at four was the central mystical experience
of her life. "Just at that moment," she said, "you know Helen Keller's
wonderful moment when she put it all together? Realizing that those
symbols meant something that I could be part of was like an act of
magic."

And how fond she was of Dick and Jane in the school readers. "I *understood* Jane," she said. "Jane was very sturdy and knew her own mind. And I loved the way that Dick was good to her, protective of her. Everyone was terribly good to everyone else. There were no bad intentions."

Carol also talked about how she found it harder to project herself into the mind of a modern woman in her twenties in *Swann* than to write with the voice of a man her own age (in *Happenstance*). When Carol herself was the age of her twenty-eight-year-old heroine, the feminist scholar Sarah Maloney, she was still in a sort of infancy, she claimed — "detained too long in childhood," as she once wrote. This despite the fact that she already had three children and was living in England, becoming a socialist.

Then she told me a little story about her slightly older brother and herself when they were children. "When we walked in the back lane," she said, "he always said the moon followed him, and then I said, 'No, it always follows me.' We paced off and we walked, and I suddenly saw it followed everybody. This was a sort of revelation." (Carol drew on some of these vivid childhood experiences for her central character Reta Winters in *Unless*.)

I thought this perception so characteristic of Carol's generosity of spirit. Her particular kind of humanity has always dazzled me. It's the foundation of her commitment to writing as a form of redemption, redeeming the lives of lost or vanished women — whether it's Mary Swann or Daisy Goodwill (in *The Stone Diaries*). Or, for that matter, Larry Weller in *Larry's Party*. She's interested in nothing less than the shape of a human life, the possibilities for self-awareness, and really, consciousness itself — the hum inside our heads. Indeed, one of the reasons that she switched from biography — early forays into Susanna Moodie — to fiction was that she felt that ninety per cent of what happens to us occurs inside our heads, and this is inaccessible to the biographer.

A few days after those first conversations, she had some more thoughts and wrote me a letter.

I've never for a minute doubted the value of women's experience. Whenever my books met with critical scorn because of their subject matter, I just shrugged. Other critical comments I listened to, but not this one. When I told you living in England made a socialist of me, I meant that was when I became active. The exact moment of enlightenment came years earlier in a high school class when a teacher explained about the division of wealth in terms of need. (This was in the McCarthy era and I was astonished that this was what the fuss was about. Why, this sounded suspiciously like what I had learned in Methodist Sunday School! And it sounded so sensible!) Just one of the many double messages floating around in those days. I think I did recognize the doubleness, but thought it ironic and funny — and couldn't get too worked up about it.

Although Carol and I never (after Vancouver) lived in the same city, we became friends, exchanging letters and books, seeing each other whenever she came to Toronto, writing and talking about books (thick letters in pre-e-mail days). In fact, she once told me that she was concerned that a big part of the way she experienced the world was through books — maybe more than other people do — and maybe there was something "substandard" about that. Among her papers at the National Library in Ottawa are her shopping lists; between the carrots and the onions are titles of books — books to read or to recommend to friends. As anyone who's read her criticism or essays knows, Carol was not only a generous writer but also a generous reader. In Winnipeg, she belonged to a book club, although that reflected her talent for friendship as much as her love of books. Despite many moves, Carol had friends going back to her childhood in Oak Park, Illinois. In her own writing, she was witty, often ironic, always affectionate, with a delicacy and subtlety of language. Sentence for sentence, she was a marvel. (I remember her telling me about trying to write a *non*-ironical story for that special issue of *Room*. With all that irony, she said, she was "beginning to get a case of lockjaw." But then she added, "You may find it a bit sappy.")

Carol was a gutsy writer, experimenting with a range of narrative approaches — omniscient, direct, fractured. When she turned fifty, her writing turned a corner. "You get older and braver," she said, "braver about what you can say and what can be understood." She was once quite tickled when someone described her work as "post-epiphanist." She was very conscious of courage — the word came up a lot — I think because it was a muscle she developed in herself. Deliberately. Heroically.

Carol cherished the virtues, the joys, and the griefs of everyday life. But she was also sensitive to the cracks in the surface — how sometimes they reveal a frightening fragility in our lives, a glimpse of darkness, but more often a moment of transcendence, something that cuts right through everyday experience in a miraculous way. What she referred to as "random illuminations": clarity, harmony, pattern, whimsy. She told me she believed that everyone has these "moments of transcendence." One of hers that she incorporated into a story ("Collision" in *The Orange Fish*) involved walking in the rain in Tokyo under a stranger's umbrella; rhythmically in step, she felt she could have gone on like that forever. "I believe in these moments," she said, "when we feel or sense the order of the universe beneath the daily chaos. They're like a great gift of happiness that comes unexpectedly." Another such moment occurred in a motel on her honeymoon, but that was all she would say.

The obverse — how vulnerable we are to loss and tragic reversal — isn't something she dwelt on. "It doesn't matter how insulated you are," she acknowledged, "you have these frightening glimpses of the utter meaninglessness of your life. It's a kind of angst when you suddenly feel that you're alone and powerless and nothing makes any sense. It's the opposite of those transcendental moments when you perceive the pattern of the universe." Such sentiments inform her characters at times — from Judith Gill in *Small Ceremonies* to Daisy Goodwill in *The Stone Diaries* to Reta Winters in *Unless*. But if Carol had a psychological blind spot, it was to depression. She could understand feeling discouraged or down but not the utter debilitation that deep depression could engender. More characteristic would be the opening sentence of *Small Ceremonies*: "Sunday night. And the thought strikes me that I ought to be happier than I am."

I interviewed Carol about virtually all her books. On one occasion, Before — in fact, just a couple of months Before — she said, "I never believed that people were formed at age seven and we'd never escape that inheritance. I think people are always changing and changing quite dramatically, and that what changes them is access to language and their ability to expand their expression of themselves through language. I always see everything through the screen of language."

In talking about reading, she said, "Reading novels is not escape; it's a necessary enlargement of my life." Typical of her range, she first quoted Saint Augustine, who equated reading a book with having a conversation with the absent, and then her own character Judith Gill: "My own life will never be enough for me."

Carol's interest in Jane Austen went back to her own childhood and her search for intelligent female heroines in fiction. Long before she wrote her monograph on Austen, she spoke at a Jane Austen conference in Ottawa. The focus was *Emma*, and she talked about "the image of the body, or rather, the lack of image of body." Her paper was subtitled "No Fingers, No Toes," because Austen "never in all her books mentions these bodily bits." As Carol wrote to me at the time, "No hips, no kidneys, wombs, shins, skin, intestines, navels either. Thank heavens someone's done a concordance, and so I'll be able to report accurately that in all of Austen there are 8 necks, 6 knees, 2 eyebrows, 10 ears, and 1 ankle, etc. Actually there are six breasts, but they all belong to men."

I loved the way Carol's mind worked. The evening prior to that last Before interview, we had an opportunity to go to a movie. I chose one that had been recommended: a wild, raucous story about gypsies in Central Europe. It was awful, but Carol was very careful, tactful about dismissing it. Finally, she asked me what was the worst thing about it. I said, "The noise." She said, "The romanticization of the emptiness of their lives."

In spring 1999, Carol won a Guggenheim Fellowship. In her application (Before), she said she wanted to write "brave and original books . . . in which readers will take pleasure." The novel that she ultimately wrote was *Unless*, her most explicitly feminist book.

EW: One of the most startling things about *Unless* is the fierceness of it. When you come across scenes of Reta and her friends at their weekly coffee gatherings, it's easy to think, for all the consciousness-raising that went on back in the sixties, things haven't really changed that much. What do you think?

CS: Things haven't really changed that much. A few big acts of legislation have made more areas of work open for women, but just a year ago, I heard [the British literary critic] George Steiner say that he didn't believe there were any women writers of the twentieth century. That gave me pause. What does he mean? He says in the nineteenth century there were one or two women, but he doesn't see women as a force in literature. Particularly in literature, I think, women have been given very minor roles, not taken seriously.

EW: Even today?

CS: Even today.

EW: You've described this as your most overtly feminist book to date. Did that surprise you?

CS: Yes, it did. For some reason I felt I could say some of the things I'd been thinking, and I was thinking about some things I hadn't thought through before. So I came to a place where I felt I could say these things. *I* was the woman in the audience, by the way, who asked George Steiner the question, What about women writers? So maybe I took the reply more personally than if I'd just listened to someone else pose that question.

In *Unless*, I did some of the things I'd long wanted to do: write about a writer, write about the love of children, the intensity of that tie, without sentimentality, and of course about the acceptance of women into literature on their own terms. I don't think this has happened, and how are we going to make

it happen? I think we're going to have to change what we think
of as literature to a certain extent in order for women to be
fully felt in our writing.

In 1991, Carol's companion novels, *Happenstance* (which follows the
life of Jack, a historian) and *A Fairly Conventional Woman* (which
follows the life of his wife Brenda, a quiltmaker), were published in
England as one volume, bound back to back. Carol was delighted
because she hated the title *A Fairly Conventional Woman*. Initially,
the combined volume was called *Happenstance*; later it was reissued
as *Duet*.

"That title [*A Fairly Conventional Woman*] has thankfully been
obliterated," she wrote me. And then, "How I loathe that title, it
hurts me to write it out. The hybrid edition came out in the UK last
year. As you can see, they made a real effort at symmetry, but then
went and put the price code on Brenda's side. Tell me what this
means, please."

Carol enthusiastically faxed me (and others) a copy of an article
from the *Guardian* called "Why men can't write for toffee." The
subheading was: "Are there gender differences in writing? Ferdinand
Mount thinks so, and he prefers women."

There are so many moments from Before that I can look back on.
Her cooking the dinner from *Larry's Party* for my fiftieth birthday in
Winnipeg. Staying at the Shields's places in France — first in the Jura
and then at "Chateau Pulitzer" in Burgundy. Writing a reference for
a Canada Council grant for a novel to be called "Flower and Stone,"
a book that became *The Stone Diaries* (*The Republic of Love* was
originally called "Bodies of Water"). The thrill of her introducing
me at a talk I gave at the University of Manitoba. Hearing her speak
at the University of Toronto campus in Mississauga, attending the
reception at the chancellor's house for her honorary degree from
the University of Toronto. Then there were the moments that she
described in her inimitable fashion: the 1993 Booker Prize party in
London (where Roddy Doyle won for *Paddy Clarke Ha Ha Ha*); their
sabbatical in Berkeley; Christmas in India.

December 1998 marks the great divide between Before and After. I was busy preparing for a major work trip to Russia when Don called. Carol felt too teary. I made only one long-distance phone call when I was in Moscow and caught Carol just as she was coming home from the hospital after her mastectomy. In the next few weeks, we talked and began much more frequent phone communication. I was number six on the speed dial, after her five children. Occasionally, she'd cry on the phone; I'd cry after we hung up. Once I established that she was still able to read, I started sending books. Thus began my role as her "official bibliotherapist," as she dubbed me. Carol wanted good but undepressing books to read. "I looked for novels that were a little more cheerful," as she later said, "and had more narrative movement to them. And characters — I always think of Darwin when I say this because Darwin is famous for doing his science work in the morning and then in the afternoon, having someone in the family read a novel to him. They would ask, 'What kind of novel? What should we read you?' And he always said, 'It doesn't matter as long as there's someone in the novel I can truly love.' So I wanted to read novels about people I could love and feel a sense of kinship with."

Some months later, when Carol started to talk about what she was going through, she alluded to these books in speeches or interviews, and I was asked to provide a list. This is it:

> Diane Johnson, *Le Divorce*
> Barbara Trapido, *Brother of the More Famous Jack,*
>   *Temples of Delight, Juggling, The Travelling Hornplayer*
> Rose Tremain, *The Way I Found Her*
> Hilary Mantel, *A Change of Climate, The Giant, O'Brien*
> Jonathan Coe, *The House of Sleep, The Winshaw Legacy*
>   *or What a Carve Up!*
> Sybille Bedford, *Jigsaw*
> Lillian Ross, *Here but Not Here*
> A.S. Byatt, *The Matisse Stories*
> Amos Oz, *Panther in the Basement*
> Ian McEwan, *Enduring Love, Amsterdam*
> Pat Barker, *Another World*
> Margaret Forster, *Hidden Lives*

Andrea Barrett, *The Voyage of the Narwhal*
Kate Atkinson, *Behind the Scenes at the Museum*

Carol reflected later on her particular experience of reading "that strange winter and spring of '99." She said, "I feel sure I read in a different way than I'm reading now, much sharper, though probably terribly subjective — more open too to new kinds of things. There those books were, stacked on my bedside table. It was just a question of taking the top one and going at it. How fortunate to be in that irresponsible position — if you know what I mean."

Less than a year after the diagnosis, Carol was celebrated at the International Festival of Authors in Toronto. I felt it was an important thing to do, so I spoke to Greg Gatenby, who agreed. Greg and I didn't want Carol to think it was because she was ill, so we went through a small charade in approaching her. It was a success. Five writers, including Margaret Atwood and Joan Barfoot, spoke. I began as follows:

A few years ago, a journalist writing a profile of Carol called me. We met and talked for an hour and then — although he certainly wasn't writing any kind of muckraking piece — he lamented that he couldn't find anything bad about her, that he couldn't find anyone who would say anything bad about her. The article didn't get published. But, I thought, there has to be something.

Ah, I thought, go to the children. *Mommie Dearest*. And that's how I found out about the wooden spoon drawer. Carol has five children. When the kids were naughty, she'd threaten them with the wooden spoon drawer. "I'm going to the wooden spoon drawer," she'd say, and they'd run away, shrieking. Sometimes she rattled the handle. She never actually opened the drawer and certainly didn't brandish a spoon.

One day, John, the eldest (and only boy), said to his sisters, "Don't move when Mum heads for the drawer." So they didn't. Carol threatened again. They didn't move. They saw an anxious look cross her face and then, sensing something wrong, uneasy, they ran off shrieking. Another time, when they were acting up, Carol not only threatened to phone Santa and tell him that they were misbehaving and undeserving but actually did. There they were in tears, and it was too late, she was already on the phone, talking.

Of course Carol wasn't always a mean mother. There was the time that the children were late getting off to school, and so there she stood beside the stove, shaking the egg timer to make the sand go through quicker, so they could finish breakfast in time. And she never told them to "go out and play." She thought that wasn't a very nice thing to say to anyone, and besides, why would you want to go out and play if you could stay in your room and read? And the children didn't have to clean up their toys because Carol thought that would spoil the fun of playing. Or, when Carol finished *The Box Garden*, her second novel, there was a scene of sex on a train: the central character, Charleen, and her boyfriend were travelling across the country. He had his finger . . . somewhere. Carol's oldest daughter, Anne, who was fifteen at the time, read a draft and was horrified. How could she face the kids at school if they found out she had a mother who wrote such smut? So Carol took it out.

During the International Festival of Authors that year, I again interviewed Carol onstage.

EW: You've talked about being concerned about — this is how you put it — "the unsettling self-absorption" that cancer had led you into. How did you escape that?

CS: Well, I don't know that I have. One of the things that worried me more than anything else is this self-absorption. Every muscle that twitches, every little pain you feel — you're always listening to your inner music and testing yourself against the healthy people in the world. I worried that this, that it would make me too self-absorbed. Part of the joy of my life has been reaching out and having people around.

This is a subject we revisited.

16 March 2001
"Am I thinking about 'it' every moment? you asked. No, but I'm mindful of 'it.' Mindful: such a useful word."

19 June 2001
"I've just finished Anne Tyler [*Back When We Were Grownups*]. I love hundreds of little bits of it — she is wonderful on hair. And children. And food. And smells. It is subversively feminist, about a woman who must be forever jollying up other people, rather like *Breathing Lessons*."

13 June 2002
"I have to organize my entropy better."

I have a photograph taken at Government House in Victoria in May 2003. I'm walking on what seems to be a yellow brick road — sunshine drenching hardwood floors — with Carol and Don. We are all smiling, though I don't think we were aware that we were being photographed at that moment; we were just entering the hall for a reception during the International Writers' Festival. For a while I kept the photo on my fridge but then it made me too sad so I put it in a drawer. But the picture was important, evidence that I hadn't been totally blind (even if I was in gross denial): that last time I'd been with Carol, she *had* been relatively well and lively. Less than two months later she was dead.

During those years when so many close to me were dying, I experienced a sort of low-grade melancholy pierced by grief. I became accustomed to staying on top of various test results and appointments, all the ebb and flow of illness. Death in no way resolved any of this, though it may have put an end to that particular pattern. It's all a subtraction, a taking away with nothing to replace it, a deficit.

30 December 2000

"Only to connect. And to tell you I woke in the middle of the night last night, reached for *Stet* [by Diana Athill] and relished that odd hour, between 3 and 4, I believe. It seemed heavenly to be carried along at that particular pace, with all that eighty-year-old tact and attention. And at the same time such openness. I'm going to take it in small, middle-of-the-night bites. . . .

My New Year's resolution is to stop shuffling along and playing the patient. I'm planning on becoming a person again."

2 January 2000

"I've been feeling more optimistic than otherwise. I wanted to tell you that I finished Lynne Sharon Schwartz's *Leaving Brooklyn* yesterday, which I thoroughly enjoyed. Her Brooklyn is certainly not the Brooklyn (*Tree Grows In*) we imagine, closer to Oak Park. The part I loved best, and connected with, came early on in the book when she spoke about always, from early childhood, being in love, and having to carry that absurdity in secret, knowing just how ridiculous it was. There was always someone, a little boy in her class or the chicken seller's son — but someone. Amazingly, she needed no response to her love; it was enough just to possess it. I have never seen this particular human rhythm (for want of a better word) described before, but I recognized it at once as something that has always been part of me."

Because Carol thought she might not be well enough, or even alive, for the publication of *Unless*, she did publicity ahead of time. I recorded an interview at her home in January 2002.

EW: Do you ever think in terms of "something *unless* something?"

CS: I never think in terms of something after this life. This is it, and this is why we have to use the time we've got to blurt bravely and get some words on paper and have lots of conversations with lots of people — I think that's very important — connecting and having conversations, that's a huge part of my life. Being interested. Somehow, I've been able to remain interested in everything that's happening, and you want to hang on to that as long as you can.

EW: As the character in the performance piece *Mortality* says, she goes "right up to the wall." It's not even a breath away.

CS: Yes. I find that a very comforting thought. If you think of death as a part of life — and, in fact, it is — it just intersects exactly with it, and it's just a breath away. It's not that big a thing.

Not only did Carol not believe in any sort of afterlife, she felt strongly that she didn't want any monuments to her death — no gravestone, not even an urn.

1 June 2001
"Here's the Karl Shapiro poem, 'A Cut Flower' [discussed earlier on the phone], which may sound depressing but which I found oddly comforting. Now I wail: Where are my bees? love, c"

A Cut Flower

I stand on slenderness all fresh and fair,
I feel root-firmness in the earth far down,
I catch in the wind and loose my scent for bees,
That sack my throat for kisses and suck love.
What is the wind that brings thy body over?
Wind, I am beautiful and sick. I long
For rain that strikes and bites like cold and hurts.
Be angry, rain, for dew is kind to me
When I am cool from sleep and take my bath.

Who softens the sweet earth about my feet,
Touches my face so often and brings water?
Where does she go, taller than any sunflower
Over the grass like birds? Has she a root?
These are great animals that kneel to us.
Sent by the sun perhaps to help us grow.
I have seen death. The colors went away,
The petals grasped at nothing and curled tight.
Then the whole head fell off and left the sky.

She tended me and held me by my stalk.
Yesterday I was well, and then the gleam,
The thing sharper than frost cut me in half.
I fainted and was lifted high. I feel
Waist-deep in rain. My face is dry and drawn.
My beauty leaks into the glass like rain.
When first I opened to the sun I thought
My colors would be parched. Where are my bees?
Must I die now? Is this a part of life?

My last e-mail from Carol:

30 May 2003
"I'm getting my senses back, reading and writing with no more
than the usual clumsiness. It seems a case of the crabby pills
and stocking other pills for the hon degree. Bless you, dear
human, for offering to read. I've just finished Jill Ker Conway's
A Woman's Education. Hot, hot here, and heavenly."

I spoke to her just after that conversation about *Unless*, and *Mortality*
was broadcast in April 2002. She didn't feel as calm and accepting as
she had when we talked. She told me, "I sounded braver than I feel
now. Tomorrow I'm starting the new chemo and then I'll really feel
lousy." I cried when I listened to the program because that April one
of my other friends was dying. Carol said, "I hope you see him off

peacefully. I wish him an easy passage." After my mother died, I got these messages from her.

20 January 2001
"Just to let you know that I am thinking of you every day and feeling how tough the first week and first month are. I did write you a note the other day, but of course didn't manage to say what I meant."

22 January 2001
"I know these must be difficult days. I suppose we have an image of ourselves, someone's daughter, someone's sister, and suddenly that is radically altered or cancelled. And then there is the change of routine, of visits and phone calls."

25 January 2001
"Just to say I'm thinking of you. Spring is coming and I think that will turn your spirits."

"Always a Book-Oriented Kid"
THE EARLY INTERVIEWS: 1988-1993

EW: Let's start at the beginning — growing up in Oak Park, Illinois, home of Ernest Hemingway.

CS: When I was there, it was an exceedingly WASP suburb of Chicago. What a place to grow up! Like living in a plastic bag. There were seven hundred and fifty students in my high school graduating class and we were all white, every one. I always knew something was wrong with it, but I never knew what it was until I went away. What was wrong was that there wasn't enough. It was all very good, it just wasn't enough. Everyone went to church. Almost all Protestant, though there were a few Catholics. That's what I thought a mixed marriage was.

I was the class poet and right through high school I loved to write sonnets. They were an attempt to use the sort of language I now despise in poetry — for example, pretty language. I do hate pretty language. One of these sonnets started out, "Satin-slippered April, you glide through time and lubricate spring days." Another one, "Oh I hear the sound of the Prairie . . ."

Not long ago, I was going through old mementoes and I found one of my poems printed on the graduation program, and it was really embarrassing. Naturally, it was in conventional metre, it rhymed and ended with "Going toward the future wherein awaits the end of every dream." And the thing is, I knew then that that wasn't true. I knew that was false rhetoric. But it was part of the rhetoric of the day. For my thirty-fifth high school reunion, I've been asked to write a new poem and the line I'm starting with is: "We were all white."

In some ways I feel my childhood was very uneventful. We had a predictable family, the usual aunts and uncles and extended relatives. There was only one death, my grandmother's. But I didn't like her very much and didn't know her very well, so it just happened.

EW: Did you live in a ranch home?

CS: No, in this kind of suburb there were no ranch homes. The houses were built around 1910; in fact, Oak Park is famous for having these lovely Frank Lloyd Wright houses, which I did not live in, but I certainly lived in a house of the period. I lived in a big old white stucco house.

EW: What did your parents do?

CS: My father managed a candy company. He disappeared downtown every day to work. For a long time, I didn't know what he did. My father had three years of university, then had to quit when his father died. My mother was a fourth-grade teacher. She stopped teaching when she had children because she wasn't allowed to continue. Then she went back after the war when there was a teacher shortage and she taught until she retired. She had two years of Normal School, teachers' training college; it wasn't a degree. In later life, she was obliged to go back and get her degree. So they were semi-educated people.

My mother's parents were born in Sweden and there were eight children, four of them born in Sweden. She was at the tail end, one of twins, Irene and Inez. It's such an exotic name, Inez, I can't imagine where they got it. She never liked it because the Midwestern pronunciation was Innis.

EW: Did you have any sense of what your parents' expectations of you were? Did they expect you to have a career?

CS: My mother said to us once — very solemnly at the kitchen table — that she had failed Latin in high school. She told us that so we would not feel, if we failed anything, that it was the end of the world.

They wanted all of us to go to university — my sister and me as well as my brother. Although I went to college and majored in English, I also got all my teaching qualifications at the same time because they insisted on that. They encouraged my brother to go into engineering — those were the days of engineering — and my sister did primary school teaching. My sister and I each had a degree, but we knew we would get married and have children. The lives of middle-class girls in my era were highly predictable, but nevertheless — and this is sort of a Depression thing — we were told that we must "have something to fall back on." No way did anyone ever think of a career.

EW: When you were young, what did you think you were going to be when you grew up?

CS: I was writing even then. I was encouraged by my teachers, and my parents, too. They were very excited when I got something in the school paper. But I never thought that I would have anything professionally published. Even though in my high school yearbook I was the one who was going to write the novel, I never believed that for a minute. I'd never met a writer; it just seemed far too difficult a thing to be. But it seems to me I was always involved with language, right from the beginning. I think it may have something to do with being short-sighted — this is just a theory. For me, learning to read was the central mystical experience of my early life. Realizing that those symbols meant something and that I could be part of it was like an act of magic.

I was always a book-oriented kid. One of the things that was important to me was story hour at the library which lasted, in our town, up until grade eight. People still told stories for older kids and I almost always went to that. That combination of drama and narrative was something I loved. We had some books at home, we had a set of encyclopedia and so on, but we didn't have a lot. But one thing I had was all my parents' old childhood books, so I read all of Horatio Alger, for example. I wish I had those books now. My mother loved *Anne of Green Gables*. She couldn't wait until we were old enough to read it. Now that I've read both volumes of Lucy Maud Montgomery's memoirs, I've realized how that coincided with my mother's own life. Was it 1908? My mother was six then, so the book was established by the time she was a teenager. I suppose that Anne was a model to millions of girls who weren't ever able to act out the kind of battles that she had.

EW: Do you think Horatio Alger had an influence on you?

CS: No. But I was certainly drawn into those books and actually — this is how random a reader I was — I even enjoyed those Dick and Jane readers. Being a middle-class child, I certainly didn't find them alien — Jane especially, with her little white socks. I *understood* Jane. Perhaps I projected onto those characters much more than was there, but they seemed like real people to me and their world seemed wonderfully safe and ordered. Probably even safer and more ordered than my own safe and ordered world.

Jane was very sturdy, knew her own mind, I always thought. And I loved the way that Dick was good to her, protective of her, so unlike most brothers. Everyone was terribly good to everyone else. There were no bad intentions there at all. It was so nice.

EW: Did that ring true to your own experience?

CS: No, surely not. It was a kind of fairy tale, even though all the middle-class signs that I recognized were there. But this sort of extraordinary goodness is very appealing to children. I don't know when those books stopped being used, but I think something was lost — this ideal world. Of course this ideal world could be threatening to people who weren't so close to it.

I loved fairy tales for a long time. Then overnight, I didn't like them any more and wanted stories, very realistic stories, about kids in school. I just tumbled into another period. We never bought books in our family, we had these books at home and no one added to that stock. My parents believed in the public library. I think I owned only about three books in my life at that time; I was never given books.

I remember the first adult books that I read. One of them was *A Tree Grows in Brooklyn*. It was quite a shocking book when it came out. Then I read a book by Edna Ferber. Once I started reading even these not very good adult books, I never read children's books again. It was like a door opening.

EW: Into a more cosmopolitan world?

CS: My own world was probably less safe and ordered than I thought it was. I don't know about my own parents' insecurities. I do know they were both timid people, so that instead of their having expectations for us, the expectations came to a large extent from the school system. Oak Park schools were very wealthy. We were all in classes of about twenty. Until I got to high school, I never had a teacher who was not an unmarried, middle-aged, bosomy woman. They were wonderful women and very caring. It was a kindly system, but limited. Imagine growing up near Chicago, just a few blocks from where James T. Farrell of *Studs Lonigan* fame had grown up. He was never mentioned in high school. I didn't even know anybody who lived in the city of Chicago, and I lived only fourteen blocks away. My mother was a Girl Scout leader and she'd take us all down to the Art Institute [of Chicago]. But I had no idea what the outside world was like. I suppose I thought that the books I read were the unreal world and mine was the real one, but in fact it was just the opposite.

EW: So you went to high school in Oak Park, and then you went away to college?

CS: Yes, as almost everyone did. It was the next step, I put very little thought into it. I just sent off for all kinds of catalogues, and I chose a school that looked like a *Father Knows Best* college — small, very conservative. You'd have thought I would have wanted a taste of the world. If I have any regrets, it was that I didn't plunge into something more bravely. Why didn't I go to the University of Chicago? I would have loved it. It was a mistake, in a way, for me to go to Hanover College. So much of it was a waste for me. I even belonged to a sorority, and I was bored with that, but I wasn't brave enough to stay out of the system. I think I'm one of those people on whom education was wasted. I was much more interested in falling in love and going to dances, although I did some reading. One lucky thing happened. I went, during my third year, to Exeter University, and it was a great surprise and wonderful to get away from the sorority house. I was in a totally different environment where we were not spoon-fed. I remember my advisor at Hanover had given me a sheet to take to my professor in England. It was huge and had little squares in which he was to give me daily grades. When I showed it to my professor in England he looked at it, then tore it into four pieces and threw it away. We were on our own in England. To go to lectures or not. People took their subjects seriously. This was all a revelation to me, that people would sit in the dining hall and talk about Christopher Marlowe. It was wonderful.

EW: You met your husband in England?

CS: Yes, he was from Saskatchewan, on a graduate fellowship.

I met him that year, but I did go back and finish my degree. I had a baby the first year we were married.

EW: I guess at this time you gave up any idea that you were going to be a writer.

CS: Except for one thing. When she first met him, my mother mentioned to my husband, Don, "I hope you're going to encourage Carol to keep on writing." Don looked blank. We were engaged to be married, and I had never mentioned to him that I had done any writing. I forgot about it for a while. I was just interested in being in love and having a house, the whole *Ladies' Home Journal* thing. That was all I wanted. I can't believe it now.

My husband remembered this, and after I had had my second child, he said, "Why don't you do something, there's a course at the University of Toronto in magazine writing." So I went to that class. I can't remember much about it except that a woman lectured to us once a week — there were about forty of us — and she had a big hat, which she never took off. She came in, lectured away, and I can remember she said, "When you send in a manuscript you should use a paper clip and not a staple." That's all. Toward the end of the year, she wanted us to actually write something and so I wrote a short story. Then I forgot about it. In the middle of that summer, she phoned and said, "I've sold your story to the CBC." I couldn't believe it. So over the next few years when we were in England — my husband was doing his Ph.D. at Manchester University — about once a year I would stir my stumps and write a short story, and I always sold it — to the CBC, or to the BBC, without too much trouble, which you would have thought would have encouraged me. In fact, I was pretty relaxed about it all, and instead of doing more, I was having French lessons and taking an interest in politics. My time in England had made a socialist of me, and when I came back, I joined the NDP and was somewhat active in our local party. Being in England turned me around a bit; I started waking up. Have you ever read Annie Dillard's *An American Childhood*? She talks about how long it takes. Her childhood was in some ways like mine, although she's younger and she grew up in Pittsburgh in a wealthy family. But there were certainly many parallels to my experience: that childhood is a long waking up; that at ten, she thinks, children finally wake up fully and stay awake. Before that you're always falling back asleep. This made so much sense to me, and I do remember sort of waking up at the age of ten, but I really didn't wake up until much later. I had a very prolonged girlhood.

EW: But you were a mother so fast. Had you always wanted to have lots of children or did that just happen?

CS: Well, the Kennedys were —

EW: But they were Catholic.

CS: One of the kids was a bit of a surprise, but the others — it seemed a comfortable number to us. I loved having children. Physically it was hard work, and I can remember being tired a lot, but I can't remember having the kind of frustrations I've read that women with young children can have. I was young and I had a lot of energy. I hadn't started really writing so I never felt, at that time, that the kids were keeping me from writing. When I got back to Canada, I thought a little about what I would do, but then I had another baby. I belonged to a "Great Books" discussion group. I was involved in my neighbourhood with other young mothers. I always resent the disparaging of coffee klatches because the women in my neighbourhood were enormously supportive of each other, in a very real sense. What else was I doing? I was always reading; even when I had all these kids I read a lot. I had this idea of going to law school; I took a few courses at the University of Manchester. I read Betty Friedan's *The Feminine Mystique* during the trip home on the boat. (Those were the days when people travelled by boat.)

Around this time, I became conscious that the women in the fiction I read were nothing like the women I knew. They weren't as intelligent. There was a real gap. And they weren't as kind. I was reading fiction where women were bitches or bubbleheads. I was reading mainly novels and non-fiction. Then I read a review of a book by Philip Larkin. It was such a positive review that I went to the library and got the book. I loved it. I thought, "Good heavens, this man is being honest." It really was a wonderful revelation. I thought, "I'm going to write some poetry." At that time, the CBC had a competition for young writers. I was twenty-nine; thirty was the cut-off. All spring, I had this little baby crawling around, and I wrote seven poems. I hadn't written poetry since those sonnets in high school. I worked and worked on these poems. It was the first time in my life that I took my writing seriously. In fact, I mailed them off the day before the deadline, and I can remember coming back from the mailbox and Don saying, "Well, it's nice to have you with us again." I must have been totally absorbed in that. I won the competition. I can remember Robert Weaver phoning and saying, "We're really pleased because none of us has ever heard of you." That led me into a period of about five years when I wrote poetry, which was an enormously happy writing time for me. I was very strict with myself. I followed Larkin's set of rules: no pretty language. Unfortunately, I also borrowed some of his despair, I think, in my first few poems. I remember my friends being a little worried about me: was I contemplating suicide?

EW: This wasn't something you felt inside?

CS: No, I think Larkin led me into this sort of perspective. When I finished a poem, I would ask myself the question — and this was something I had never done in my writing before — Is this what I really mean? I was very severe about it. I worked;

when I think of the hours I spent revising and getting it just right, it gave me such pleasure. I felt as though I were making these lovely little things, these little toys.

EW: And then you tripped over Susanna Moodie. How did that happen?

CS: When we went to Ottawa and my husband joined the University of Ottawa, I realized that I had this free tuition. Being very thrifty about these things, I decided I'd better take advantage of it. I signed up for an M.A. in Canadian literature. I started in 1969 and there were hardly any mature students in the system. The graduate advisor took me aside and said, "We have not had much success with part-time, married women." I didn't care. A couple of years later, women were coming back in droves and they were having enormous success.

One of our essays was about Susanna Moodie, and I decided I would do my term essay on her. Even so, when it came to the thesis, I was going to do P.K. Page because I liked her poetry. I even interviewed her when she was in Ottawa, staying at the Château Laurier. I talked to her about some of her poems and I asked her what one of the poems meant. She said, "Oh, I haven't the faintest idea." At this time I was rather severe about these things, and I thought, If she doesn't know what it means, why am I going to try to figure it out? Since then, I've met all sorts of poets who don't understand their writing, and I've written things myself I don't quite understand. I thought, If I'm going to do this, it had better be an act of love, something I really want to write about. I remembered the essay on Susanna Moodie, and I decided I would look at the work we never look at in Canada — all those horrible novels she wrote.

EW: What was it about Susanna Moodie that attracted you?

CS: When I went through all those old novels there were re-curring themes, and the most interesting was the male/female one. Moodie always pays lip service to the supremacy of men, but if you look at her novels, without exception, the men are weak and the women are strong. You get a recurring tableau of the supine male and the woman nursing him back to health, you see this again and again, all the way through. I think it's utterly unconscious.

Another theme that I found — I didn't do much with it, but I would if I ever wrote about her again — is the theme of sibling rivalry between her and Catharine Parr Traill, who was a little older and more beautiful. So that's there in all her novels. But most of my thesis was uncovering this male/female thing. About the feminization of men, how men learned; how boys' spirits were broken. Her children's stories are horrifying in this way.

EW: You've said that you didn't think of yourself as a feminist in those days — the early seventies. How did you become a feminist?

CS: I can remember when I was first married and living in a little apartment in Vancouver. It was the first week of our married life and I was in the kitchen cooking and I thought, Why am I doing this? We've never discussed it. But it was only a flicker. The process was very gradual; I never went through those consciousness-raising sessions, I was never a member of a feminist action group. A lot of my experience of what a woman's life could be came from reading fiction, not from reality. Reading Betty Friedan's *The Feminine Mystique* made an enormous difference to me. I went to hear her speak at the University of Ottawa. I didn't have many models of women who were doing much.

I've always been interested in the lives of women and I've never doubted that they have value. But I can't really remember when I became a feminist. I think I'm one of these women in between, too late to be an old-style woman and too early to be a new-style woman. I'm always going to defer to men to a certain extent and I can't get over it. I regret that.

EW: How did you come to start writing your first novel, *Small Ceremonies*?

CS: I was offered the first job of my life. This is when I was still writing my thesis. I became the editorial assistant on a scholarly quarterly for two years, *Canadian Slavonic Papers*. With small children, I did this job at home in my own little work room. The journal was edited at Carleton so I'd go in occasionally, but most of my work was done at home. It was what people call a jobette. I did that for a couple of years and then I finished my degree [in 1975]. I had all this material left over from my thesis on Susanna Moodie that I couldn't use because it was too conjectural. So I thought I would try to do something with it. And that became *Small Ceremonies*.

EW: But you'd never written a novel?

CS: Oh, yes, I had. I had tried to write a novel during the early seventies, when I'd dropped out of university for one term. It was a literary whodunit. And I sent it to a few publishers and they all returned it, but they wrote very nice letters. So I thought I would try again. *Small Ceremonies* went very easily. I wrote two pages a day, every day, and at the end of nine months, I had a novel. And it was published just as I wrote it. It was so easy to do, it was wonderful, it was a very happy time.

EW: When you wrote *Small Ceremonies*, did you know what you wanted to say in your writing?

CS: I wanted to write a novel about a woman that I would rec-ognize, who had a reflective side to her life. I wanted to show a woman who had good friends. I was always surprised that in the books I was reading the women didn't have friends. In Virginia Woolf's books, such as *Night and Day*, I did sometimes see women friends but very seldom good friends. I wanted to have children, I wanted that context. And I wanted to use some of the Susanna Moodie material. I have a very strong sense of connection with the past. I wrote about this sense of history in another novel, *Happenstance*; I think it's something that some people have and some don't, like having an ear for music, which I don't have at all. But I do have this other feeling where I connect with historical events. I feel myself a part of it. I'm surprised when I meet people who don't know where on the timeline things occur. I'm interested in the connection we have with the past, and particularly with women in the past.

EW: *Small Ceremonies* is about a biographer; do you know what it is about biography that interests you?

CS: I think it's the only story we've got. The only story with a nice firm shape to it is the story of a human life, but so much of it is unknowable. I like fiction because fiction can go where biography can't. It can go where most of it happens, which is inside the head. It's where nine-tenths of your life goes on. So I can see the weaknesses of biography, but I'm very attracted to the shape of it. I love novels that cover very long periods of time so that a person's life can be traced.

One of the interesting things about Susanna Moodie is the silences in her work, the things she doesn't say. You can try to fill in those spaces, but how do you retrieve that? How do you retrieve someone who is dead and try to build up with the nib of your pen a personality who was, in a sense, voiceless about things that mattered?

EW: In filling the gaps, how do you know what's authentic?

CS: I don't know if it's authentic. But I do think that the things she leaves out are the authentic parts of her. And the other parts are not. It's like reading a negative. It's marvellous. And in a way, it's a little bit like the resurrection of Mary Swann in *Swann: A Mystery*. How can you ever know anything about a person who's been so effectively erased from the world?

EW: So you just sent off *Small Ceremonies*?

CS: I sent it to three publishers — McClelland and Stewart, Macmillan, and Oberon — the people who'd sent me the nice rejection letters before. They all sent it back and I was fairly discouraged. But we were getting ready to go to France so I was distracted by other things. I thought maybe I could cut it up and make short stories out of it. Ever practical.

EW: Reminds me of my mother making pillowcases out of old sheets.

CS: That's an excellent analogy. Then I went to the bookstore to look for more publishers. I sent it to McGraw-Hill and they eventually accepted it. It was wonderful. The week I turned forty, they phoned to say they were going to take the novel, my two professors said they were going to publish my thesis, and we were on our way to France — all in one week.

EW: Did you then think you were going to be a novelist or was this simply a novel you had written?

CS: I thought, I'm going to be a novelist all my life.

EW: Did you write while you were in France?

CS: I started *The Box Garden* the first or second day we were there. I had a kind of postpartum feeling and I was missing the people in *Small Ceremonies*. I remembered that there was a sister I'd alluded to a couple of times. I thought maybe I'd start with her. It seemed so easy to flow into it because I already knew the family. I knew the set-up. Again, it went quite easily — not quite as easily as the first one, but it was also finished in nine months.

I had a lot of doubts about certain things that I did in that novel, even as I was doing them. I should have listened to those doubts. The editor of *Small Ceremonies* had told me that there was not much happening in that novel. I took this as a set of instructions that I should make something happen in my next book. That's why I decided to put a pseudo-kidnapping and the police in *The Box Garden*. You can imagine how much I know about these things. I wouldn't do that again.

EW: Your next novel, *Happenstance*, was an apparent shift, a shift in locale to Chicago and to a male point of view.

CS: One of the things that puzzled me about the two books I'd already published was that they were being called "women's books." So I decided to pick up the gauntlet and write something from the male point of view. I wrote it in the third person, though, instead of the first. That book took me a little longer. I had a few problems with it. I started writing in the wrong place. With the other books, I started on page one and worked my way through — exceedingly methodically. With this one I went a certain way and realized that the children were going to be more important, so I had to go back and introduce them.

Then I had to do a kind of re-plating of the story when I was finished because I realized I'd made Jack into a kind of buffoon. I don't know how that happened. I wanted him to be a man who was trying to be good in a world in which it's not always easy to be good. And feeling his way and being occasionally foolish as we all are, but not continually. I felt I was mending — I had this darning needle and I was going through the book to keep the tone toward him the way I wanted.

EW: Did you find it difficult to write from a male perspective?

CS: I didn't think it would be. I really do think that men and women are more alike than we admit. I think men speak differently, they use language differently, so I was trying to pay attention to that. Also the withholding of language. I was very interested in friendships between women and friendships between men — what do they mean? What do these silences between men mean? Does this mean that the friendships are superficial? In fact, I never quite resolved that one. I think my position in that book was that no, the friendship was genuine, but there was a lot less shared.

EW: Why did you locate *Happenstance* in Chicago?

CS: I was going to write a short story about this man and I was going to set it in Chicago. McGraw-Hill tried very hard to get me to change it to Toronto because they didn't feel that this typified an American family — it was far too gentle. That was ridiculous because I'd grown up in a family just like that. My father never fired a gun in his whole life.

EW: Then you turned around and wrote a book from the point of view of Brenda, Jack's wife.

CS: People asked me whatever happened to Brenda when she went away, so I wrote *A Fairly Conventional Woman*, which was great fun. I love writing about the fifties and trying to recover the way we thought during those years, and I loved fitting those two novels together. It was like a game. I remember once the editor phoned and said, "Hey, you left out the cheese sandwich they ate at their meeting." So I put in the cheese sandwich. I had also changed her dress size, so I had to fix that. I loved working on all the timing and details. I was also very interested in the way we share memories, how different they are. And the silences between people, the acceptable silences between people. I wanted to write about two people who were more or less happily married, but who were in fact strangers to each other and always would be, and about the value of the strangeness.

But the main thing that I wanted to write about was a woman's discovery that she was an artist and what that does. Nothing had prepared her for this sense of herself. Most reviewers missed that and they thought it was about a woman on the brink of an affair. That was the red herring. But a lot of people bought it, and I have to take responsibility for that myself.

EW: There is an uneasiness expressed by a number of your women characters — these are women who are mostly okay, but they're not as happy as they think they should be. There's a sense of something missing. Is that a starting point for you?

CS: I suppose it's a universal perception, that kind of existential angst that we all carry around with us like a big lump. I love the Chinese expression "double happiness." That's what we really want: double happiness, not just single happiness. And we can't get it. A lot of people say I write optimistic and happy books. I'm not always optimistic and certainly not always content, but relative to many people I must be; otherwise I wouldn't be hearing this all the time. You can't live in this century without having a sense of loss somehow.

EW: We were talking about safe and ordered worlds, but there is in your books, *Swann*, for instance, surface order and safety, and then there's a glimpse of — horror is probably too strong a word for it — but something dark and chaotic underneath.

CS: I think that's true. It doesn't matter how well insulated you are, you're going to get glimpses of that chaos. They're frightening. It is a kind of angst when you suddenly feel you're alone and powerless and nothing makes sense. It's the opposite of those other equally rare transcendental moments when you suddenly feel everything makes sense and you perceive the pattern of the universe. I think we all get a few of these moments. I'm very interested in finding language to record them. They are what poets are always trying to write about. What Byron called "the everlasting moment."

EW: Is it in a sense part of why order and safety are important to you, to keep these kinds of glimpses at bay?

CS: I think so, but also so we can function, so we can lead creative lives. I think creativity flourishes in tranquil settings. I always loved that bit where Virginia Woolf talks about the need people have for stimulation, for travel, and how writers need the opposite of stimulation. What the writer needs is everydayness. They need to be in the same chairs day after day, with the same books around them. The day I read that was just before Don and I were going off to Ghana for two weeks. I was in a funny place. I love to travel, I love these experiences, but I was nearing the end of writing *A Fairly Conventional Woman* and all I wanted to do was write that book. I resented having to go away and be stimulated. As a result, I took no notes when I was in Ghana and I'm sorry about that now. But I wasn't really there.

EW: Do you take notes when you travel?

CS: I usually keep a travel diary; I'm not very good at keeping a journal, although I've been getting better at it. I think it's valuable. Two years ago, I started keeping a journal of my reading. What I really wish is that I'd kept a journal when I was young; I can't really remember what it was like to be young.

EW: Do you have demons? "Glimpses of chaos" made me think of demons.

CS: Time passing is one. Aging. Sometimes I have days when I'm reconciled to aging, others when I don't want any part of it. Inactivity. I suppose I had my first taste of writer's block last year in France. It wasn't a complete block. I kept writing, but it was just as though I were sweating. It just came out in little drops instead of the way it should come out. It lasted about six weeks. I don't know why it happened — perhaps, and this is being very kind to myself, because I was trying to do something harder. I had to think more about it; it just came more slowly. I thought I'd resolved a way of working that was useful to me, writing a certain amount every day and revising it carefully, going about it in a careful way. I just couldn't write that way, but it passed.

EW: Your fiction took a more experimental turn in 1985 with *Various Miracles*. What happened?

CS: I discovered the old storyteller's voice, the omniscient narrator. I'd never tried it before and I wanted to. I thought I would write a book of short stories, because you're not bound to one particular voice. I could tell stories from close up or from far back. I wanted to tell stories from children's points of view, I wanted to do all the narrations. The other thing I realized as I wrote those stories was that I could get a little bit off the ground and let the story find its own way. I decided to let that happen, let it go where it seemed to go, even if it didn't make any naturalistic sense.

EW: You've spoken of numinous moments. Do you think of yourself as spiritual or religious?

CS: I'm not religious, though I was brought up in the Methodist Church and for a while I went to Quaker meetings. I do believe in these moments, though I don't know where that belief comes from. Not from any spiritual centre. I think it comes from the accidental *collision* of certain events. I think the English language is very poor in its vocabulary to describe mysticism, so a lot of this never gets talked about. Or only clumsily, or only by people that we think are perhaps only marginally sane. Or it's sometimes discoverable through poetry.

EW: Does it come from a yearning for some kind of connection?

CS: I don't know if it's so much a yearning; I think it's more of a celebration. When you experience one of these moments, it's like a great gift of happiness. Of course, everyone would like the moment to go on and on and on, like an endless orgasm. But it doesn't. It doesn't happen again the next day or the next. You can't order these things into being. You can't say, Today's the day I'm going to have a transcendent experience.

EW: You've written about the reassurance of domestic life, about couples and families, but I don't think I've ever come across your arguing more persuasively on behalf of love and coupledom than in *The Republic of Love*.

CS: In that novel I was interested in what had happened to the whole idea of the love story, the great seizure of passion, the story we read from the nineteenth century. Something has happened to the love story; it's become a little bit flabby in our century. It's been done to death by pop-song lyrics, greeting-card verse, and the cynicism that's collected along the way. Nevertheless, I still think it's the thing that distinguishes a human life. I think it's what makes us larger than we are, it makes us better than we are. It's everlastingly mysterious, though.

So I wanted it to be a book about what love means at the end of our century, what the search for the other means. That the love story of serious fiction isn't really in the mortuary drawer, as it were, that it's still happening all around us. This novel gestures all the time toward the nineteenth century and the idea of the romantic story, in which you have a cycle of attachment and then a disruption of that attachment and then a reconciliation.

EW: You call your novel *The Republic of Love* because love is democratic. As you say, it's not a kingdom; almost everyone gets a chance to say "I love you," and to hear those words said to them.

CS: That's always surprised me, thinking about it, because here is this precious commodity, love, this mysterious commodity. Nevertheless, it is very widely spread; almost everyone gets a chance to experience it, to love, to be loved. Not all these relationships work out, but everyone gets a little bit of it.

EW: This seems to be a republic where people often lose their citizenship.

CS: I do have quite a bit of faith in the endurance of love. We always hear about the divorce statistics, for example; what we never hear about is the endurance statistics, which are also amazingly impressive. If we look at it the other way around, say, fifty per cent of marriages survive. That seems an extraordinary achievement. None of that ever seems to find its way into fiction, the endurance of love. It sounds stunningly boring, of course, when you talk about the endurance of love — maybe there's a better phrase — and no one pretends that an enduring love is uninterrupted. I think love has always been disrupted and renewed. But do you remember what the Venerable Bede talks about? Pre-tenth century — it's a wonderful image: that our life is such a little thing, it's like a bird in the darkness suddenly finding a way into the banquet hall and flying through it and looking down at all the banqueters and then flying out the other side. I always thought how much better it would be if there were two birds flying together.

EW: I want to turn to your latest novel: why did you decide to call it *The Stone Diaries*?

CS: That was a major compromise between me and the publishers. We had a terrible scramble for titles right after the book was finished. My original title is so unmemorable that I can't remember what it was, but we came up with this. I also liked "The Stone Curtain," but no one else did.

EW: I'm asking because to me it has quite a lot of resonance with the stone working its way through the book, in terms of people's names and quarrying, and it appears everywhere, but diaries . . .

CS: Yes, "diaries" is problematic because it's much more of an autobiography than a diary, and of course it's an *unwritten* autobiography — she never sits down and writes. This is the autobiography, or diary, that she carries in her head, this construct of one's self that we all carry around with us.

EW: I like the idea that this novel is an unwritten autobiography.

CS: Which is actually written by me, so it's this postmodern box within a box within a box, but the inside box is empty. This is the image I had of it all the way through.

EW: Tell me about her, this autobiographer, Daisy Flett Goodwill. It is a kind of biographical treatment of her life, which spans most of the twentieth century.

CS: I didn't start out with a full idea of who she was. I started with this tiny little baby, and as the novel went forward, starting with chapter one, chapter two, chapter three — it doesn't always work out so neatly — she grew in my mind, and very gradually she became this person.

EW: Did you have the circumstances of her birth in your mind? They're very dramatic.

CS: Oh, yes. For years I have collected newspaper accounts of women who were pregnant without knowing they were and then suddenly — wham! — from stomach ache to childbirth. Of course, I was also interested in women dying of childbirth and why they did. There are all sorts of reasons, but to have a baby in 1905 was almost like entering a lottery: your chances of losing your own life were very great. And I was interested in my mother's generation, not so much my mother's life as the world that she inhabited. I'm told this is something that happens to people at a certain age: we want to go back and feel out the surfaces of our parents' lives.

EW: Let's move forward into the century. You started with 1905, day of birth; you're moving into, as you say, chapter one, chapter two, and you lay the book out that way.

CS: Yes, the writing of the book went well, because I had this structure right away. I was going to lay it out in the usual biographical chapters — childhood, youth, love, marriage, motherhood, and so on, right down to death. Ten chapters. That seemed to make the writing of the novel easier, to have it compartmentalized. But I wanted all the titles to be just slightly askew so that each one reflected not what was in the chapter, or what would traditionally have been there, but something quite other. The image I had in my mind was that I was slicing into this life at more or less approximate ten-year intervals and seeing what was there, like a still life in a sense.

EW: You said you didn't know, yourself, who she was when you began. How did you figure it out?

CS: These things are hard to pin down. In many ways, she is like so many women of this century who became, in fact, nothing. Their lives did not hold many choices. They were this huge army of women, they were mainly voiceless, they were defined by the people around them. And that became the trick of writing this novel, to write a biography of this woman's life — but it's a life from which she herself is absent.

EW: You've worked with this before — the idea of the invisibility of a life. I'm thinking of *Swann: A Mystery*, where there are all these people, this little battalion of researchers and friends and scholars and whatnot, trying to piece together a woman who is essentially invisible: Mary Swann. Is it only women's lives that are invisible in this way, that go unrecorded?

CS: I think this is true of women's lives much more than men's. You only have to read the obituaries. There you see men defined by their professions or by the organizations they belong to — president of an insurance company, or the Knights of Columbus, or something like that — but women's lives are almost always defined by the people around them — wife of, mother of, loving grandmother of — and I think you disappear a lot faster if you don't have any of your own identification tags. Women do these disappearing acts. I'm sure there have been loads of women this century who haven't even had a social security card to remind people of who they were. And you certainly see it in graveyards, you see "Loving Wife" and sometimes not even her name. Men disappear too, of course. I have this impulse to see fiction as a form of redemption, to redeem what otherwise might be lost.

EW: You have said that Daisy's inability to express herself is the true subject of *The Stone Diaries*.

CS: Not only her failure to express herself but her failure to *want* to express herself. It's an absence of wanting. All she does with her life — this is her life's work — is fill in these biographical gaps, which she does through acts of imagination. For example, you can't *know* your own birth or your own death, but you can imagine it. In the case of my own birth, my mother used to talk about it and it used to embarrass me terribly. She would say, "Oh, you just slipped out like a lump of butter." I used to say, "Oh, Mother! Don't say that!" I know some of the other facts of that day, but the rest you fill in, I suppose, if you think about these things at all. In Daisy's death scene, in her final coma, she is simply imagining the kinds of things that people will say after she is dead, or what will be left over from her life; these little bits and pieces of lists and scraps of conversation form part of her death scene.

EW: Is that why when she dies her last words are "I am not at peace"? Because her existence wasn't authentic or actual? I don't really know which word to use.

CS: I see the book in a certain way as the nineteenth-century novel turned upside down — those novels where the whole book is a search for meaning, and then meaning is discovered. But in this case, it's a search for meaning or authenticity and it isn't found. That's the modern part of the book, I suppose.

EW: Although when I finished the book, I didn't feel sad. There is a poignancy, there is pain recounted, but at the same time, paradoxically enough, it feels as if she had a full life.

CS: Yes, I felt exactly the same way, and this is, as you say, a paradox, that in fact she did have most of those strands that we want in our life, but she didn't know it.

EW: Your earlier novel *The Republic of Love* was a fairly unabashedly romantic love story in some ways. Love in *The Stone Diaries* is something else, although a number of characters speculate about it. At one point Daisy's husband thinks about his life with Daisy and comes to conclude something like, "Love is a word trying to remember another word." What does that mean?

CS: Romantic love, which I would love to think happens to everyone, doesn't happen to Daisy Goodwill. It's another misconnection. She misses it in her first marriage and she misses it in her second.

EW: I think one of the saddest lines in the book is where, near the end of her life, she recalls that no one ever said to her those words, "I love you, Daisy." There's something terrible about missing that.

CS: Whether or not Daisy knew real love in her life is in some ways immaterial. What matters is that she didn't know that she knew real love; there was no resonance from it, if it did occur, and this is how she sees herself, and so this becomes the reality, of course. And what does it mean? When I was writing *The Republic of Love,* I asked all my friends about love and their feelings about it, but we were never able to actually pin it down. So what do we mean by love? In terms of vocabulary, it's simply in a basket with a lot of other words that are exaggerations or diminishments of that word.

The Stone Diaries isn't a feel-good book the way *The Republic of Love* was. Who's to say why? It's probably because I'm a little older, I've seen a little more, and one does inevitably get a little darker as one gets older.

EW: One thing that's very distinctive about this book is the fact that Carol Shields the author is having a lot of fun, "just fooling around," as the narrator says. She talks about a doctor "whom I'm unable or unwilling to supply with a name." And at another point she asks, "Have I told you such-and-such?" What are you doing here?

CS: I'm reminding myself that I'm writing this and Daisy Goodwill isn't, although she is the "I" of the narrator. She looks ironically at her life occasionally, but she's not a particularly ironic woman. And it *was* fun. I have to tell you that, like most writers, I find writing hard work and what I love is *having* written rather than the actual writing. But I loved writing this book. I never wrote anything with greater happiness. I'm not quite sure why. It seemed to me it was about something important and it seemed to be going well, and I gave myself permission to do just what you're mentioning, to have a little fun with it, and to recognize the fact that the novel form — my favourite form, my chosen form — is a lot roomier than I'd ever thought. In fact, you can put anything in it, you can stretch it in any direction you like, and more or less get away with it.

Letters, 1990 - 1994

Winnipeg
28 August 1990

Dear Eleanor,

I was just delighted with your loan of Annie Dillard's book [*The Writing Life*], and have already noted that one of the chapter epigraphs is by Julian Barnes: "It's easy, after all, not to be a writer. Most people aren't writers, and very little harm comes to them." Which I think is wise and also pretty funny. The day after our conversation I had a note from Brenda Riches (who lives in Regina — perhaps you know her) who said she'd just read a book she knew I'd love: *Flaubert's Parrot*. Hmmmm. Naturally I began to wonder if I'd judged him too harshly, knowing how circumstances contribute to the degree with which we can open ourselves to a book. I found my old journal with my notes, and I do seem uncommonly vexed. "Infuriated" is what I've written. Because it begins with a dazzling piece of description that makes you think you're in the hands of a great storyteller, and then it's all downhill. Because he insults and belittles and bullies the reader (really? — I've forgotten). Because he's aggressively cute. Because he leans on the greatness of Flaubert. Because he's intellectually shallow but with high pretensions. Because more than half the book is quotations. Because the skinny little story he keeps promising is a bore (can't remember). And because the book's been such a success! Wow, pow — what a dose of vitriol. (There's also a note to the effect that I should have been warned off by the back-of-the-book endorsements of Fran Lebowitz and John Irving.) How odd to think this flat faded ink (1985) was poured out with such fury. I wonder why. A headache maybe, or rainy weather.

Thanks too, Eleanor, for the interview with Ivan Klima, particularly interesting, I thought, for his remarks on the dangers of commercialized culture, also on Havel. I'll pass it on to a Czech friend I'm going to be seeing tomorrow.

I reread *Emma* this summer and underlined her famous "One half of the world cannot understand the pleasures of the other." (Of course the truth of this strikes me every time I drive by a golf course and see those FOOLS out there having such a GOOD time.)

One week before term begins. I'm doing my usual one course. This year it's something called Intermediate Writing and Research, which I've taught four or five times before. It's open to anyone in the university who wants to improve their writing, and in some ways it's rather a relief from teaching Creative Writing. By the way, have you given up entirely the idea of teaching at Victoria? I don't know how you could bear to give up what you have in Toronto.

Love, Carol

Winnipeg
27 September 1991

Eleanor — a quick note to thank you for the reviews. The [Josephine] Humphreys book sounds most interesting (she *would* have to be beautiful too), particularly the ending with two marriages and two marriage renewals. My new book — the one that's coming in Feb., ends with one marriage and one renewal, and so should have half the impact. These things are in the drinking water it seems. (By the way, Margaret Atwood talks in her new book — somewhere — about "geology is destiny." Yours. Which I've also used, thank you, but in its "geography" form.) I've finished the two articles, Jane Austen and Margaret Laurence (for a commemorative volume for Simone Vauthier). I've decided I don't have the bones for academic writing, too much glue and equivocation and timid forays into other people's theories. Enough.

See you soon,
love C

Montjouvent, France, 39270
3 July 1992

Dear Eleanor,

Mail in Montjouvent is always welcome. (On the odd mail-less day the postman knocks anyway and gives me his condolences.) We've been here for three weeks and settled into our country rhythm — walks, little projects in the house, reading (especially reading) and writing. I find it hard to write letters home since our life here is so uneventful, that is, it does not have the kind of "news" that can be easily reported. And yet the days seem full. The new novel (about 4/5 there) is at a self-conscious sludgy spot, and so I'm giving it a day's rest and plan to do some serious cooking instead.

Please let me know your response to George Steiner, a person who interests me a good deal. How does it feel to be in conversation with the world's most intelligent being? — though you suggest some of your dialogues with European males are more like lectures — I *know* the *feeling*!

Met Anita Brookner. We had a good long talk about books, about writing, about what one *can* write about. She does only one draft

— this amazed me — and when her editor suggests a change she feels she "simply can't" — almost as though it might betray the writing or be unfair to the reader. Interesting.

Enjoy your westcoast holiday. (No, I haven't read the new Ellen Gilchrist, am reading elderly paperbacks only.)

> love
> Carol

Winnipeg
14 September 1992

Dear Eleanor,

I'll make this a quick note since I want to walk over to the post office before it gets dark. I mentioned this title [Anne Lamott, *All New People*] to you some time back, but my daughter Cath never returned my copy — and I didn't like to ask her again — so I bought this for you at a library sale. The first part is rather new-agey, but it improves.

Did you get my telephone message re: the Steiner interview? Superb. Bits of it have been going through my head all day. (I loved being quoted.) No, indeed it did not feel like a conversation, you really did all the listening, but it was a joy to hear someone so articulate and, I think, honest. (Every sentence he uttered had a firm period.) He persuaded me it really was outrageous for the BBC to "send" him at midnight, the nerve! And I loved what he said about us all becoming wanderers, though I'm not sure it's true. Nor do I know what he meant about Canadian universities in decline, especially when I think of the about-to-retire deadwood at the U of M English Department and the brilliant graduate students coming along . . .

Our summer was a joy. And I wrote exactly 100 pages. And gained two kilos which I'm now about to walk off.

Better hurry. Hope all is fine with you. It's ages, about a year,

since I saw you, but I hear you so frequently on the radio it doesn't
seem that long.

love
Carol

Berkeley, CA
2 December 1993

Dear Eleanor,

Greetings from California, another sunny day, oh dear. Don and I
have been suffering from travel-blur, but here we are at last, installed
in our loft in Berkeley, actually just outside Berkeley city limits. It's in
a '30-ish factory building in an area which is just getting into gentri-
fication. This particular loft-apartment was put together by a young
couple, a sculptor (he) and a photographer/painter (she) who have
recently split up after untold hours of restoration work. The light and
space are magnificent, and there are little "art" touches everywhere,
curious objects and arrangements, balls of sagebrush, glass jars with
objects in them (our favourite has a tiny wooden ladder climbing up
its side), bird nests. We have the Pope himself as a fridge magnet.
Our third-floor bedroom is huge as a ballroom, with the bed floating
in the middle of it and an old fashioned four-legged bathtub floating
off in one corner. "She" has placed a circle of candles around this
tub for candlelit bathing, and I've taken up this new activity and
recommend it. However, living inside someone else's sculpture isn't
all bliss. No towel rails, for instance. (Don can't get over this.) Dust
— old dust — in all the little cracks and on the overhead beams. And
a kitchen that's unworkable. But I have a little work station on a sort
of mezzanine overlooking the kitchen and studio, airy and cozy at
the same time. Here's where I intend to spend my days while Don's
at the university, dabbling in math at the moment. After Christmas
we move to a house which is more conventional, larger, and full of

California comforts, including a hot tub on an open deck. (My, I seem to have a fixation on tubs these days.)

There's lots going on at Berkeley, plays, readings, lectures, all sorts of events which are open to anyone. A few weeks ago we heard a lecture series by Jonathan Miller who is a visiting professor here for six weeks. He talked on the history of hypnotism, was amusing, erudite, charming, solid — and we got to meet him at the reception afterwards. He's writing a book on this subject, and plans to go into the theories of mass hypnosis, the way crowds behave. In addition to all this activity, Berkeley has all sorts of cappuccino places, bakeries, restaurants, bookstores — and the sun has shone continually since we've been here, though now we're getting into the odd rainy day.

Now follows a brief Booker [Prize] Report. Brief because it seems so faraway, dreamlike, though it was only a few weeks ago. It was both dazzling and awful. Extraordinarily sophisticated and curiously boorish. The Guildhall, where the awards dinner was held, is utterly beautiful — and the people, men in black tie, women sparkling with jewellery, and wearing mostly black too, were also rather beauti- ful. (I bought new earrings for the event, my only investment in beautiful-peopledom.) We sat at round tables for the dinner, trying to ignore the TV cameras which seemed to be everywhere. Cigars were passed after dinner. Now that's pretty boorish. The speeches had little cynical edges on them, past grievances trotted out, not quite "nice." (The head of Booker Inc. — an immense, red-faced man — informed me that Winnipeg was a very, very dull place, and I was quite lost for a reply. "Is it?" I said. Lamely.) Our table was Fourth Estate [English publisher of *The Stone Diaries*] people with some *Guardian* people too — they are a major investor in the firm. I thought the head of Fourth Estate, Victoria Barnsley, would burst into tears when Roddy Doyle's name was announced, but I have to admit — ever the pessimist — I'd expected it. By the way, Roddy Doyle and I both forgot to bring our invitations to the dinner and had to go into a little anteroom to be "interviewed" before they'd let us in. Security at the dinner was extremely tight since Salman Rushdie was there — looking, I might say, exactly like Salman Rushdie. Someone whispered into my ear after dinner, "Mr. Rushdie would like to meet you," and then led me through what I thought was a crowd

of friends, but was, in fact, a crowd of bodyguards, four men deep.
We had a nice chat about the Future of the Novel, and he said he
was in the middle of mine. I didn't know whether to believe this or
not, but decided I might as well. I also met Stephen Spender, 84,
erect and handsome still, and his wife, who looks like an El Greco
ghost, very old, very stately — they both told me they were rooting
for me, though I think they put it more elegantly. After dinner I met
Margaret Drabble; we had a pleasant chat, very polite and friendly,
though I don't think we said anything memorable to each other. All
quite marvelous, so that I almost forgot I'd lost. I also met all the
other nominees briefly, including Caryl Phillips, who gave me a stiff
hug and whispered something about the tyranny of colonialism in
my ear. A sort of rollercoaster night, and, suddenly it was over, and
I was on the way to California. Then back to Toronto. Then back to
California. Back to normal, whatever that means. I think it means
being able to formulate my own breakfast and knowing where I am
when I open my eyes in the morning.

I'm looking forward to the Bobbie Ann Mason; I've read her
previous books with interest, but without being gripped. Do you
have the sense she's writing about a world that isn't her world, a
whiff of condescension? At the moment I'm reading — for review
— Frederick Busch's new selected stories, *The Children in the Woods*.
I love the looseness of his prose, little scattered sentence fragments
that manage to connect without cuteness. Speaking of being gripped,
I loved the last Mavis Gallant story in the *New Yorker* — it too was
full of daring little loose bits and rubbed along beautifully — and the
Paris she wrote about felt exactly right.

Now Eleanor, I do want to thank you for your piece in *NOW*, but more
than that, to echo my thanks at the GG [Governor General's Awards]
— you have fed me courage all along. You'll deny it, but it's true.

Maybe you'll get out this way. We're going to India December 25
– January 19, but otherwise will be here.

Peace and blessings in 1994. Keep me up to date on your wanderings.

love
Carol

Berkeley CA
Sunday 30 January 1994

Dear Eleanor,

I'm exactly in the middle of *Feather Crowns* [by Bobbie Ann Mason]
and loving it! I especially like the way she takes her time, just letting
the story unroll as the quints get through those early, endless days.
I think — don't know how she did it — she's managed to produce
an enduring image of each of the five. And the scene of the train
stopping and the people flowing in! — wonderful. I do thank you
for sending it and changing my mind about her.

We are going to hear Roddy Doyle speak in a Berkeley bookstore tomorrow night. And tonight we're going to the Black Oak
Bookstore, just around the corner, to say hello to Margaret Atwood,
who is doing a signing only, not a reading. (Her big event, apparently,
was last night in downtown San Francisco.) Yes, I do indeed think
Ved Mehta is an odd duck, particularly his attitude/relationship with
women, though I loved his early books. I even liked their flatness. His
more recent work shows him, I think, as not being very self-aware. (I
saw a similar lack of self awareness in V. S. Naipaul's *The Enigma of
Arrival,* which I read this summer, so perhaps it's something Indian,
being confessional without declaring it or even realizing it.)

We're just back from an early morning walk, a stop at a local shop
to buy yesterday's *G&M,* and a visit to one of our favourite cappuccino spots. We're determined to enjoy our California time, which is
speeding by. (Did you ever hear of anyone on sabbatical who did not
complain about too little time and too little accomplished!)

We opened our gifts on Christmas Eve. Sara and a friend were
with us, and also the friend's brother and his wife, so we had a re-
spectable gathering. But it was distinctly unChristmassy to be getting
on an airplane at dawn the next morning and heading off for India.
It is a hard country to visit in many ways, but overall I came home
with the sense that it had been one of the great adventures of my life.
The sight of poor mothers with malnourished children (I couldn't tell
if these children were 6 months or two years) invaded my nightly

dreams, but there is much that is beautiful in the society. We always felt safe, and certain of everyone's goodwill. I had expected to feel appalled 24 hours a day, but this just didn't happen. We loved the openness of the people we met, and their willingness to engage us in conversation. Our last week in Kerala was splendid. A friend (he was a Ph.D. student in our department last year, writing his thesis on Bob Kroetsch) arranged our touring for us and came along. This included a visit to the U of Kerala's Canadian Studies section where I gave two informal lectures on Canadian women writers. The high point was a visit to the very tip of India, the village of Kanyakumari, where three oceans come together, the Bay of Bengal, the Indian Ocean and the Arabian Sea. We sat on the beach and watched the sun set (along with about a thousand other people, all of them silent) and then got up early the next morning to watch it rise, from the roof of our little hotel, everyone with bedsheets draped around them to keep off the chill. We saw temples and palaces and the Taj Mahal and Nepal and Benares (where our hotel caught fire) and where we took a boat out into the Ganges to watch the pilgrims and yogis, and the cremations and people thwacking their laundry on rocks. As you can see, my impressions are unsorted and also overwhelming. Perhaps some perspective will arrive as the experience fades. Along the road we saw women banging rocks with hammers, making gravel — consider that whenever your job seems monotonous. And slapping cow dung into patties and putting them in patterns on the sides of their houses to dry. While we travelled I read Rohinton Mistry's Bombay novel (which made perfect sense there) and V. S. Naipaul's *A Wounded Civilization*, and a novel of R.K. Narayan's. Don and I, with diligence, stayed perfectly healthy the whole time, though we certainly ate some odd things. Once we had lunch straight off a banana leaf, no plates, forks, just fingers. Delicious. To think we almost didn't go. . . . But we both think we must now settle down and live an orderly life. I'll be working on a play for Prairie Theatre Exchange in the next few months, and then the full film script for *The Republic of Love* (the next funding plateau has been approved).

I haven't begun to tell you about our funny house here. We've never seen such an array of electrical gadgets, and I'm terrified of the stove, it has a dozen different "programs." But it's time to be brave and stir up some lunch. I haven't read John McGahern, though I fully intended to after meeting him two years ago at Harbourfront. Courtly would describe him. And a little austere. What do you think? You mentioned Clare Boylan. I know her as a reviewer, but are you saying she writes novels? I don't know them.

Everyone writes us that Toronto has had a harsh winter, so I hope your Florida sojourn gave you a good break. I'll be there in early April, the first week, the 5th I think, to give a reading at The Book Company. I know you don't like readings, but maybe we could have dinner together before. Or coffee after. Our daughter Anne is moving to Kamloops from Richmond Hill, Ontario, today, as a matter of fact, a new adventure for them.

> Hope all's well —
> love
> C.

Montjouvent, France, 39270
11 July 1994

Dear Eleanor,

A Monday morning in Montjouvent. Don is working on the masonry in our *cave*; I'm doing odds and ends, keep running out and measuring the growth of the two grapevines we've planted; the tendrils have been growing one and a half inches per day, which seems hardly possible.

Many thanks for your note of congratulations, and for the page of *Middlemarch*. The quote is beautiful. The optimism of the Victorians! — who would dare to speak today of the "growing good of the world." We must put this on our list of IMPORTANT ITEMS TO DISCUSS. My calendar says you'll be arriving on the 10th, around 2:00, and that you have a good map with Montjouvent on it. We'll be watching for you. We'll have to talk nonstop since we must leave early on the morning of the 12th in order to get our rental car back to Paris for the following morning.

Our days have fallen into a pleasing rhythm, though I suppose it would sound dull to anyone else. I still take my daily walk, always the same 4 kilometre route, since Blanche Howard once told me that if I made my walk as regular and automatic as possible that I'd be free, then, to think of other things (higher thoughts?) — and, in fact, I think this is true.

Our big news is Don's being made Dean of Engineering — he was ready for something lovely to happen to him, I think, but very surprised nevertheless when the news came. There is a cost: they want us to cut our summers in France down to one month, but we think we can perhaps nibble away at that during the five years of the appointment. (In my first book, *Others*, there is a poem titled "The Dean's Wife." Never in a million years did I think I would become one.)

Our retirement condo purchase in Victoria has gone through, and it seems strange to me to think that we'll be moving in at the "turn of the century," such a beguiling phrase. And we'll be so old, oh my.

I'm into my major summer project, which is Eudora Welty. I have four books to review, one rather plodding memoir of her (she is still alive, as you know), two of her novels and a collection of her book reviews. At first I thought a collection of book reviews would be of no interest to anyone, but, in fact, it gives a compelling profile of her life. She reviewed books, both important and marginal, for fifty years, and this somehow "places" her in the century. And her application to the books she reviewed says so much about her and the liveliness of her intelligence and the courage she was capable of — she was not at all the isolated Southerner I had imagined. I had not read much of her before now, but these days I'm living insider her head. I'm afraid Don will soon weary of my "Eudora believes — " or "Eudora once said —"

I haven't even mentioned the fête and paperback launch in England or the week's teaching in Paris, but both went well. Signing books in Cambridge, I met three Winnipeggers in the queue, which

I found oddly thrilling. (This tiny world.) And in Paris we met and spent some time with Peter Kurth — do you know his biographies? Anastasia, Dorothy Thompson, etc. He's rather bitter about American culture, but very amusing and bright. All these adventures seem far away as we tend our geraniums here in remote Montjouvent. Five more weeks.

See you soon —
love
Carol

"The Arc of a Life"
LARRY'S PARTY
TORONTO, OCTOBER 1997

EW: I want to start by asking you the same question that I asked A.S. Byatt when she published her first novel after *Possession*. I know it's not exactly the same, but like her, you became an "overnight success" with your last book, *The Stone Diaries*, which won the Pulitzer Prize, the National Book Critics Circle Award, and the Governor General's Award; which was short-listed for the Booker and so on; a bestseller in virtually every English-speaking country, on the bestseller list in the *New York Times* and in *Entertainment Weekly*. How has it changed your life?

CS: Actually, it hasn't changed my life very much. I still live in the same city, Winnipeg. I still live in the same house, with the same person, the same friends. My daily routine is very much the same. I get more mail, but I've always loved getting mail. And I get more phone calls, people wanting me to do things. I have to juggle a little bit more, but I think I'm learning to do that.

I haven't felt — and I may be very naive about this — but I haven't felt pressure with this novel, with its acceptance. For one thing, I think you only get this once: the novel that wins the prizes and hits a nerve. And no one is more surprised than writers themselves when that happens.

But I've always believed that every book is a separate endeavour, and it really, truly comes out of a separate segment of your life; when you're thinking about other things, your mood is different, you're committed to other concerns. I think *The Stone Diaries* was rather a dark book. This is a much lighter book. I needed to write a lighter book.

EW: Why? I can remember, when you talked about *The Stone Diaries* being a dark book, you said, "Well, I'm getting older. Maybe as you get older, you see things a bit more darkly." So, what's happened?

CS: Maybe I did think that at the time. But I didn't feel that as I wrote this book. I think it has its dark moments, and Larry Weller asks all the major existential questions in this novel, such as How did I get here? Am I doing the right thing? How do I cope with this enormous confusion in my life? That's a part of it. But I wanted to write a different kind of novel, with a different trajectory, I suppose. I'm not sure why. Maybe these things are a question of extending and then withdrawing, and extending and withdrawing, and who knows where the next one will go?

EW: In writing about Daisy Goodwill in *The Stone Diaries*, you said that there was a sense in which you wanted to redeem her unremarkable life with the lives of ordinary women, as with Mary Swann. Why did you decide to write about a man in *Larry's Party*?

CS: Well, I didn't exactly *decide*. I didn't know what to write about after I finished *The Stone Diaries*, and I spent a couple of years not writing about much of anything. I did articles and book reviews and smaller projects. But I was having lunch with some of my women friends one day, and we got onto the topic of what must it be like to be a man today. And I thought, This is interesting, and it's something maybe I'd like to write about. Men have always been a mystery, the great mystery for me, the unknown. I don't understand men. I don't know how they think, what their bodies feel like to them. So why not spend some time considering that mystery?

EW: This is a mystery, we should add, that you've been living with quite closely, having been married for more than forty years and having a son.

CS: Yes. And a father and a brother, a few male friends, not too many. Nevertheless, it is a mystery because I think the way one talks to men is different. It's getting not just to that body, which is always going to remain a mystery to us, but getting to that interior monologue. What does it sound like inside those men's heads? It's a risk, and I understand now why there aren't many women writing about men, or many men writing about women, because it *is* so risky. You can get it wrong so easily.

EW: In the acknowledgments to *Larry's Party*, you write, "Thanks to a few men who have offered suggestions." What kind of research did you do?

CS: Nothing very methodical. This probably sounds as though I did a poll. I asked a few men that I knew what it was like to be a man today. Some of them went straight into their jocularity mode, and I knew they weren't ready for this. But others, three or four in particular, really reflected on the question and gave me, I thought, heartfelt answers. I also felt when I talked to them — and I was very touched by this — that they seemed to be grateful for this conversation, and that it was a conversation they had not had before. I was grateful to be having it too — a little piece of the mystery opened up, but not much.

EW: Several years before *Larry's Party* came out, you published a short story called "Larry's Jacket." Did the novel start as a short story that wouldn't leave you alone?

CS: Yes. In fact, I wrote the short story not thinking of it as a novel, but it was about this time that I decided I wanted to write a book about men, what life was like for men now at the end of the twentieth century. I was thinking about a likely person to write about, and then I remembered Larry and his jacket, and I thought, Maybe I'll start with that, something I already have a little bit of a grip on.

EW: You've written from the point of view of a man before in *Happenstance*, your third novel, and, in fact, you once said that, of all your characters, it was with Jack, the historian at the centre of that novel — Jack, the observer — that you most identified. Do you identify with Larry at all?

CS: Oh, yes, I do. I wrote *Happenstance* in the late 1970s. It was published in 1980. It was a different time for men, I think, quite a lot simpler, and even Jack Bowman, the hero, hadn't quite been touched by what was about to come for men. I feel very affectionate toward all my characters, men as well as women. Larry grew with me. He's younger than I am, of course. He was born in 1950. So it takes him through forty-seven years of his life and ends in the present day. I felt that I moved with him from his being a young man of twenty-six to forty-six. He's a rather gentle person. Someone suggested to me that he's a bit of a wimp, and I think this was said because I'm a woman writing about a man. If I'd been a man writing about Larry, they might have said I was very sensitive to that particular side of a man's nature. But it made me think that probably — I think I'm right about this — that in our heart of hearts, we are all wimps, at least for one minute out of every hour.

EW: I've always felt that, beneath any kind of confident ex-
terior, there is a quivering mass, regardless of how confident
things appear. But I think you're probably getting that accusa-
tion because Larry seems to be such a passive character. Things
happen to him.

CS: He lets his life happen to him in a sense. He's carried along
in the stream of things. I suppose I can only say that my own
life has been something like that. I think most lives are. There
are people who have a certain aptitude for aggression, who are
actually self-determining. We read a lot of novels about these
people, but how many do we meet in everyday life? I don't
think there are that many out there.

EW: In Larry's case, if anything, mistakes happen to him. Even
in his career, he becomes a florist instead of repairing furnaces
because the college sends him the wrong forms, and even furnaces was his mother's idea.

CS: Yes. Well, random accidents — I think all our lives are
shaped in that particular way.

EW: It's interesting. In writing about Larry, you've chosen what
could be called an ordinary kind of person. He has a remark-
able aspect, his making of mazes, which we will talk about.
But he is above all an ordinary person. Do you have a sense of
wanting to redeem him?

CS: I suppose that I do. I wanted to write about a decent man
because I think a lot of our literature in the last few years
has not focused on the decency in men. Men have become
the great bumblers, in very much the same way that women
in the 1950s were. I grew up with all those old stereotypes:
the mother-in-law, and the woman driver and, of course, the
dumb secretary, the inept teacher, the giggly nurse — all those
women. I think I bought into all that. I thought, Well, this is

the way the world is. Half the world is capable, and the other half is not very capable. That's changed very slowly, but I think that men are now in the position that they are the ones who take the pratfalls.

EW: And have given it to themselves. I'm thinking in terms of anti-heroes . . .

CS: Have they given it to themselves? Now, that's a very interesting question, how that shift took place. I'd have to think about that. I don't know if it has been self-inflicted, that image. But I didn't want this man to fall into that mould, and I felt that, when I did my final, final, final draft, I was going over it with this little piece of sandpaper and taking off the tips of those places where I was laughing at him just a little bit. I didn't want to laugh at him. I wanted to love him.

EW: The first words of the book are "By mistake." It's intentional. You're striking a theme here.

CS: Of course, yes. His whole life is a series of mistakes, a random coming together, accidents of various kinds: the way he meets his wife — both his wives, I suppose. In fact, all his major decisions come through the drinking water, they arrive through the window. He doesn't set out claiming, This is going to be my life, this will be the pattern of my life. In modern parlance, he's not a Type A, thank God.

EW: Now, another thing you write is "A jacket's a jacket," but it's obviously so much more than that to you and to him. Can you talk about that?

CS: Why would I say "A jacket's a jacket"? Because underneath the rhetoric of this novel, there's another rhetoric, and that is guy talk. This is a guy thing: "A jacket's a jacket." That's part of this male way of speaking, and I was after that a little bit. I was trying to pay attention to guy talk and how it works, how superficial it is, how emotionally dishonest it is.

EW: I remember when you talked about *Happenstance*, you felt that it wasn't that male friendship was necessarily more shallow than female friendship, but the way they talked was.

CS: Yes. Talking in metaphors, talking through the vocabulary of sports or cars. That's another sort of male gossip. We talk about women in their circles of gossip, but when men engage in this kind of gossip, it's passed through these other metaphors. I thought, Well, I have to try and get to some of that, so I spent a fair amount of time, while I was writing this book, listening to how that operates. And it's interesting, it's enlightening, it's sometimes discouraging, but I think I understand it a little better.

EW: That chapter is called "Fifteen Minutes in the Life of Larry Weller, 1977." Later in his life, Larry is known to many more people, although he's never quite world-famous, but why is this particular fifteen minutes in his life your starting point?

CS: I suppose in a way, Eleanor, it could have been any fifteen minutes. You could take any slice. But I wanted to show him when he was young, when he had very few cares, when those cares lay very lightly on him. When he suddenly throws that jacket off and allows the spring air to come at him, he exposes himself to it in a way that I thought of as, I suppose, somewhat emblematic, that he was just going to let whatever came at him come. So in a way, that's not being passive. It's making a choice to be open to your own history.

EW: It's a funny way of looking at passivity. You're going to be open to what happens to you. It's still happening to you, but you're going to be more actively open to it than letting it just hit you. So Larry decides to ditch the jacket, even though it feels so good, because it isn't him?

CS: It isn't him. It's going to create problems for him. It's going to be a barrier. And he has, at that moment, decided that he's just going to let his life come at him.

EW: In his forties, Larry does end up with that kind of jacket. Does it suit him then?

CS: More so. And probably this has to do with getting older. And, of course, I suppose, in terms of plot, this is the only plot that really interests me, this plot which is the arc of the human life. I'm not interested in other kinds of adventure plots or holy grail plots or climbing-the-mountaintop plots. I'm interested in that arc of aging: growing older and then, of course, the shadowy end of life, illness and eventual death. Now, this novel, of course, only takes Larry to the age of forty-six, so to use the metaphor of the maze, he gets to the middle of the maze, to what they call the "goal." This is maze talk. That's the word they use. He gets there, but now, of course, it's not an ending, it's not a happy ending, it's a resting place. Now he has to get out.

EW: It's a happy middle, if not a happy ending.

CS: It's a happy middle, yes.

EW: Larry's two wives effectively force choices upon him, and they're very different. They seem to be almost from different generations, or at least different classes. Dorrie, the first wife, starts out selling cars, and Beth is an academic. How is Larry changed by these women?

CS: He first marries an inarticulate woman. He, of course, is an inarticulate young man. And that is mostly the problem between them. Then he marries a talky, talky, talky woman, and, as you say, it does force other choices on him and opens him up. I think both these wives, in a sense, have a good influence on him: learning about women. He, of course, is changing. And this is the part that I'm always interested in: how characters change and how they often act inconsistently. When people teach creative writing courses, one of the first things they teach is that you must keep your characters consistent, and this is bad advice because human beings are not consistent. In fact, the very moments that we're most interested in are those moments in which people act inconsistently, out of character. They suddenly leap up, become larger, in fact, than they really are. I'm interested in those moments.

So his wives open him up to different worlds. One is a very contained world. One is a larger world in which he is not always comfortable, but eventually he finds where is he comfortable. Every novel that I love and am interested in is about this, is about an individual finding his or her true home. It is the journey, and you can go right back to *Ulysses* to track it. I think this is what fiction is for, and what it's about. Think of Jane Austen's *Emma*. Where does she belong? She has to find herself. Fanny Price in *Mansfield Park* is even more displaced and has to find her true home.

EW: Tell me more about what the idea of finding your true home means.

CS: I'm thinking of this word "home" metaphorically, but it's where you belong, where you understand the signs, the place where, in fact, you have always been destined to be. I think that you can be born in the wrong place, and you have to somehow move in this circular or linear journey — I don't suppose it matters — but it's often quite a long journey to find this place where you are at rest with your body and, of course, your mind.

There are novels where that journey is incomplete, where that place is not found, where there is a detour, a change of direction from outside or inside, but that place is never reached. I guess, in my own books, I have been much more interested in completing that journey, but I understand this other indirection that leads people to places where they don't want to be.

EW: Is it only in books that you find this?

CS: No, of course, no. In life as well. We can't see the direction we're going most of the time. And there is a place in the novel where Larry is talking about maze theory, which can get very technical and mathematical, by the way. But he just points to the very simple observation that if we look down on a maze from above, we can see the pattern very quickly. We can see the direct path through, the most economical path. But we can't see that while we're in amongst the shrubbery, and, unfortunately, that is where we spend most of our lives, in the shrubbery, unable to see over those tall walls.

EW: When Larry, at one point, says, "You can only get a clear picture from above," someone compares this to the godlike position of the novelist and being able to see everything from above.

CS: Oh, I remember that part. We used to think that God could see all these patterns. I suppose the novelist, in a sense, is in that position.

EW: Do you think that people's lives really are about moving through a kind of maze, following a puzzling or branching path that the maze offers?

CS: I think, in a way, it's a very apt image, that our lives do work this way, that we all make mistakes, at least wrong turnings, and have to back up and go in another direction. We don't even know what we're looking for, of course, because this is part of the mystery of mazes, that the goal is an unknown quantity. At Hampton Court, it's two spindly looking trees — rather disappointing after all that effort. But there's always a goal. We don't know what it is, and that's the interesting part; in a way, the journey is a mystery too, and the end of the journey is . . . I suppose, Eleanor, I do think that our lives are like that, that we don't ever quite know where we're going. I suppose there are people who sit down and make a plan of their life: where they want to be at age thirty, where at thirty-five, and where at forty. I've met a couple of these people, but I think they're extraordinarily rare. It certainly isn't the way that my life has moved along. I think we're moving along a kind of tunnel of time or through a maze of time, and there's no going back.

EW: But do you see a pattern in your own life?

CS: Looking back, I can see some patterns. I suppose I do. I've always felt that my life is in chapters, one chapter closing and the next one beginning: the chapter of being a kid and going to school and discovering poetry and all the things that were important to me as a child; and then the chapter of early marriage and motherhood. That seemed to be over pretty quickly. And then trying to start writing, being discouraged, but not fatally discouraged, and continuing, having a little bit of encouragement and moving on and writing different kinds of novels. And the novels I wrote in my forties belong to a different chapter than the novels I wrote in my fifties. I suppose, when you think about the passage of time, I never feel morose about this because I always think that these new chapters offer something new to me.

EW: You said you can see the pattern looking back, but if I asked you what chapter you're in now, what would you call it?

CS: Let me see. Where am I? I think probably, strictly speaking, I would be at the end of middle age and maybe at the beginning of being — what do we say? — an older person, and I don't know — I can't imagine — what that's going to be like. I'm just arriving there. I'm interested in other forms of writing now. I'm very interested in essays, writing about writing, writing about literature. I hope to write another novel and would like to see that happen, but I'm also open to new things now.

EW: It's interesting, your talking about seeing your life in chapters, because each chapter in this book, *Larry's Party*, describes Larry's life from a different angle, and it picks up a theme and traces it through his life: Larry's love, Larry's folks, Larry's work, and so on. Why did you want to tell his story that way?

CS: I always like to think of the structures of novels while I'm writing them, and usually I get a kind of concrete structure, and it helps me. It's for me — it's not for the readers — to hold this thing in my head for the two or three years that it takes to write a novel. I wanted a linear time structure in this novel: twenty years in fifteen chapters. I didn't want twenty chapters because writers never want to be seen as too schematic. So I skip a year now and then. But I also wanted a cross-structure, I suppose, a vertical structure. At one point, Larry's father has a CAT scan — I've seen photographs of CAT scans, and I think they're quite beautiful, transfer slices of human tissue — and I thought, I'll do that with Larry's life. I'll just take a slice out now and then. And so I chose these different components of a human life: his folks, his work. I wanted to talk about words, his words, his relationship with language, because language frees him to a very large extent. There's a chapter about his clothes — "Larry's Threads," it's called — a chapter about a period of illness he went through. So I had these two structures working together, cutting across each other. And in the end, I felt that that was an appropriate structure because if there's one thing I've found out about men — or, rather, have had confirmed, something I suspected — is that men tend to live lives which are a little more, on the average — I have to quantify here — more compartmentalized than those of women. Whether this is Darwinian, whether it's something they've learned, I don't know, but it seems to me that they do function this way better or differently than women do.

EW: You even have a chapter called "Larry's Penis," which includes a list of descriptives for it, which I won't make you read.

CS: Thank you.

EW: But why this inventory?

CS: You can't write about a man without writing about this central organ, which really, I think, does lead men in all sorts of directions. Why the inventory? I think it's rather extraordinary that there are so many euphemisms, and I was curious about them. I'm curious about folklore, so this is a kind of folklore of the penis. Some friends told me some names. I knew some, of course. I consulted a dictionary of slang, which offered a few more, very arcane ones, things that I don't think we use anymore. It's curious how many — far more euphemisms than you might believe.

EW: Although in a sense and, I guess, not surprisingly, Larry's own exploration of this is refracted through women, especially his second wife, Beth.

CS: Yes. She was probably the first person he was ever able to talk about it with, this strange creature, this puppyish little creature that has travelled with him all his life. And what is his attitude toward it? I don't know the male attitude, but I took a guess on this one and hoped I got somewhere close to the truth.

EW: The central metaphor of *Larry's Party* is the maze.

After years of being a florist in Winnipeg, Larry becomes an internationally known designer of mazes. What is your own experience with mazes? What do you feel like when you enter a maze?

CS: I went to Hampton Court years ago and was totally disoriented and actually was one of those people who, after a while, crept underneath the shrubbery to get out. I felt hemmed in. I have a poor sense of location; I'm easily disoriented spatially.

But when I went to England about four years ago, I went to a village called Saffron Walden. We were walking across this village, across a field, and I suddenly found myself standing in a medieval turf maze — not a hedge maze. It's something that is actually cut into the turf, but it's still a pattern. It's very clear. It's medieval, mysterious. I just felt transported by this experience. The theory about these particular mazes — and there are quite a few of them in the UK — is that they were a kind of elaborate flirtation game between maidens and young men, and they ran around in the maze, very much as we did with fox-and-goose tracery in the snow. It's a game. Mazes, for all their serious theories — and there are many of them — are, I think, games, elaborate cosmic toys. People have always loved them. They've existed in every culture. They go back to prehistory. They are carved into the earth, into stone, built up as gardens. And why? It's a great mystery to me. I love the theory that some people have — and this would apply to pavement mazes in French churches (Chartres Cathedral is the prime example) — where those pilgrims who were unable to make the journey to Jerusalem in the Middle Ages instead made that journey in microcosm on these floor mazes in the church. There's something very contained about that theory and something that I feel I can understand, in a sense; there's something rather humorous about it, too. But people think of them, as well, as the journey of life toward death. Some Asian mazes are seen as a journey toward birth, the nine months before birth, which I find interesting. But I think they're just quite a lot of fun, and we should never lose sight of that aspect of them.

EW: Larry is granted a few transcendent moments, flashes, where he sees the world clearly. One is the transformative experience he has when he visits his first maze, the 1690 maze at Hampton Court in England. Are these moments of grace or epiphany like the heart of the maze, the goal?

CS: I think they are, or maybe you have a sense that you're on the right path, somehow you've taken the right direction. And I've always loved writing about these moments, not just in this book but in my other books — the idea of transcendence, where somehow the plan of the universe becomes clear, or where we have an intimate connection with someone after a long silence, or where something happens that uses us up completely. Somehow, these are the very moments that we don't often speak about to other people, but I think it's important, if we want to hold onto them, that we somehow verbalize them, articulate them, either to ourselves or to other people — to hold them still in a net of words so that they can serve us, because I think one of these experiences, one transcendent experience, will get us through a lot of uneventful time.

EW: I like the image of holding them in a net of words because it seems, by their very nature and their evanescence, that as soon as you try to ensnare them, that's when they evaporate.

CS: Yes, they do soon evaporate, very quickly. It's hard to get them back.

EW: Larry goes along with his life, but at one point — and, in fact, it's when he's most successful professionally — he's sadder, and, as you put it, he's lost the trick of keeping track of himself. What happens here?

CS: I think this is part of the aging process, this growing older, this going through the arc of our lives. When we're young, we're taking our pulse every day — aren't we? — and seeing where we are. And then we forget to do that, and I think we go through long, dense periods without much self-comprehension. That's a part of it. And why does this happen? I suppose we're too busy, we're too self-satisfied, we become sure of ourselves, and we forget about this other part, the part that measures who we are and where we are, positioning ourselves, in a sense, in the world.

EW: But as a result of this, Larry becomes very unsure of himself. It feels like a mid-life crisis, but I couldn't really get a grip on what it was. Maybe it's because he couldn't get a grip on what was really bothering him. What *was* going wrong?

CS: I think probably he has always been someone who feels that he's been lucky. And if you come from a certain temperament or a puritan background, you feel guilty because you're lucky, and you also doubt that you deserve that luck. I think all these things assaulted him at about the age of forty. And, of course, he particularly despises a mid-life crisis exactly when he is programmed to have a mid-life crisis, and he simply doesn't want to acknowledge the fact that it has arrived precisely on time.

EW: *Larry's Party* is organized like a kind of maze. You circle back to some of the same details or previously covered ground. There's a chronological momentum, but it almost seems secondary. Now, you've given your characters interesting professions before, such as an expert on mermaids or even here a student of women saints. At what point did you realize that your form was going to so closely resemble your content?

CS: I think I must have been in chapter three when I realized that each of these chapters was, in a sense, a small maze that Larry enters and then exits at the end, so the structure felt right for the material. Getting him in and out of each chapter was the trick.

EW: Toward the end of the novel, Larry recognizes that in getting older we witness the steady decline of limitless possibility, which is what we've been talking about. But in a way, it would seem that, both for Larry and for you, getting older has produced more possibilities.

CS: Oh, I don't know about that, Eleanor. This is easy to say about someone else, but I don't think it's something that one feels about oneself. We have ideas about possibility when we're younger, and they don't have anything to do with writing ambitions or anything else, just human possibilities. And I think that there is a moment when we know that we're only going to go so far, we're only going to do so much. This is something that I think we come to at different ages, but it has to do, I suppose, with being in touch with your reality base. I think we don't dare get too far from this, from what is going to be possible for us in our lives.

EW: You have a celebration of a life, Larry's actual party, at the end of the book, and it reminded me of when you used to bring together whole gatherings of people: in *A Fairly Conventional Woman*, in *Swann*. This is on a different scale. But what attracts you to this group portrait?

CS: Actually, there are parties in all my books, and I hadn't realized this, but it was pointed out to me by a very astute critic, who tracked the parties right back to *Small Ceremonies*, where there's a kind of suburban buffet supper. I love parties, and more than the parties, I love the *idea* of parties. I love the idea of people gathering under a roof, strangers or friends or both, where there's a flow of food, a flow of talk, movement, human movement, where certain possibilities are produced that don't occur in our non-party lives. I suppose this is very primitive. It goes right back to those early feasts and primitive celebrations, that there is a need for people to come together to be other than what they are. I can always remember my parents' parties when I was a child and how I would listen from upstairs. I could hear them laughing — these would be bridge parties mainly — and I could hear my parents sounding younger and happier than I ever imagined them to be. I suppose they were their party selves, and maybe they were their real selves — who knows? I didn't know. But I knew there was something enchanting about this idea. And I can remember coming down in the morning, and sometimes the bridge tables would still be up, and the little dishes would have a few scattered cashews left, and I would find this exotic. I had a sense about parties, and I've always produced a steady run of parties in my writing.

EW: I was thinking about this in terms of reinforcing Larry's passivity; it isn't even his idea. It is actually his current girlfriend who suggests this party and brings all these people together.

CS: Yes. But the minute she suggests it, he latches onto it. He decides he wants to have it, and he wants to have it because it is going to offer him a dramatic confrontation that he, in fact, wants. And it is also going to offer me, the novelist, a dramatic confrontation that I want, so I felt it was the right time to throw this party.

EW: In giving Larry, as we've said, a happy middle, if not a happy ending, something happens that offers him this possibility. Why does he deserve all these second chances?

CS: Why does anyone deserve a second chance? I don't know if I can say any more than that. It seemed like a natural progression, given where he was in his life, for something like this to happen. Actually, I was just reading an article yesterday in the *New York Times* about the current vogue for noir, for blackness, for despair. I know people who've gone through periods of despair, and they all tell me there is nothing there, nothing to be gained. So, I thought, Good things do happen to people. Sometimes people get what they deserve, and I wanted Larry, probably because I was fond of him, to have what I thought he wanted.

EW: Early on, you have a line that worried me because it said, "Love was not protected. It sat out in the open, like anything else."

CS: Yes. Of course, I think that is true, and it's never fully protected, is it? It can be taken from us at any time.

EW: Can you talk about what it means that love is not protected, that it's out there in the open like that?

CS: Love is a gift, isn't it? We can't expect to have it all our lives. When it comes, we want to hang onto it. But in a sense, we have no right to hang onto it, and it is not ours to hang onto. It's vulnerable, it's fragile. It's like those flowers in Larry's florist shop, I suppose. They're utterly fragile. Daffodils have a three-day life. I was surprised to learn that this was true, in fact. I thought it was just that I wasn't good at looking after my daffodils, but I was told by a florist friend that that's all they give, that's what they will give you. I think that love is not a stable place. It's open to all sorts of other forces. That's what I meant. We think, when we have it, that we'll have it forever, but I don't agree. And that's my piece of noir for today.

EW: You talk about Larry and his consciousness, that his name rhymes with "ordinary" and that the whole world may be full of guys named Larry. His name, Larry Weller, reminded me also of Sam Weller, from Dickens's *Pickwick Papers*, who is full of good humour and good nature. Did you want to evoke that resonance?

CS: No. I wish I could claim that insight, Eleanor, but it didn't occur to me until afterwards that I'd completely forgotten about Sam Weller. It's a rather common Canadian and American name.

EW: I have to ask you: *The Stone Diaries* had all kinds of fake photographs and family trees. Here, there's just one on the title page. Who's the kid in the high chair?

CS: I don't know. I wish I did know, and my publishers would be happier if I knew too. I just found this little photograph amongst our family photographs, so I assume it's someone related to me. The full photograph, which isn't reproduced here, is of a little boy whose high chair has been carried out of doors, so in the background are these big, leafy trees. It's rather surreal looking. But what I really love about it is the way his tiny little hands are curled onto the tray of the high chair, like little clamshells, and the look on his face is one of perplexity and fear, and to me, it looks as though he's saying, "I'm going to have to grow up and be a man — whatever that means."

EW: And, of course, that is the question that you ask. Someone in your novel asks, "What's it like to be a man in the last days of the twentieth century?" Did you come up with an answer at the end?

CS: I didn't come up with an answer, although I may have come up with a few shady insights. I think a lot of men are feeling threatened. I think they're feeling disoriented, puzzled about what it means to be a man. What is the definition of masculinity? What are the comportments for today? How do men interact with women? Partly, it's the business of political correctness and what one does or doesn't do. But mainly, it's this re-evaluation of what it is, what it means, to be a man.

Letter, 1998

Winnipeg
31 August 1998

Dear Eleanor,

Welcome home. Hope you stagger through the first few days. I am
so pleased and grateful you'll do this [Guggenheim] reference — a
bother, I know. They will contact you directly, with my proposal
attached.

I thought *Cold Mountain* [by Charles Frazier] was quite an ac-
complishment. The man is a demon researcher, little details. And one
gets a strong sense of the roughness and incivility of society in the
South. I have some reservations. He killed quite a lot of people on
his way home — didn't keep count, but a lot — and seemed utterly
unreflective about this. And I think he gave his heroine a degree of
liberality that would never have occurred. Also did a tease in the last
section. Enthralling, though. The book brought to mind the question
I've been mulling over all year: why do people read novels?

Delighted you'll be part of the Humber evening and, yes, we can
take some time, maybe for dinner.

love, carol

"Art Is Making"

EW: There isn't a lot of violence in your work. Mary Swann gets killed, and there's a kidnapping in *The Box Garden*, a plot device that you later said you regretted. But in *The Stone Diaries*, a man falls to his death out a window, on his honeymoon, when his wife sneezes, and it's comic. And in *Larry's Party*, a woman accidentally poisons her mother-in-law with home-canned runner beans. These are often passages that you choose to read from the novels. What's going on?

CS: You either see the world as richly comic or you don't. But I do think that every woman who has ever done any home preserving feels that she is going to poison someone. It's a universal fear that we're going to cause death. Daisy, I suppose, never knows whether she sneezed her husband to death or not, but it's our human condition to assume some guilt in the face of others' tragedies.

EW: I know you like to write about the cracks in the surface — how sometimes they reveal a frightening fragility in our lives, a glimpse of darkness. But more often, they're moments of transcendence, something that cuts through everyday experience in a miraculous sort of way, what you've referred to as "random illuminations." Can you talk about how these have operated in your own life since, mercifully, the tragic ones haven't.

CS: I've always believed — and this might be a sentimental notion — that each of us is given a number of these moments of transcendence. There's a terrible story about a New England housewife who was washing dishes one night and she happened to notice that on her wrist the soapsuds had gathered and they were catching these little rainbows of light. Suddenly it seemed to her that her whole life came together and she understood the meaning of the universe. So she called her husband into the kitchen to share this moment with him, and he immediately phoned for a psychiatrist and an ambulance. This is the problem with these rare moments of transcendence; they're very difficult to shape into language that doesn't sound utterly insane. I think this is why we don't always even recognize them, let alone share them. We don't know what brings them about; usually it's a strange combination of things that come together, but I think they should be savoured so that we can call on them in moments that are less than transcendent.

EW: Can you give a for instance in your own life?

CS: I suppose I can. This is one I used in the novel *Small Ceremonies*. I was in a train station in Britain and a man, clearly deranged, was running through the crowd. He was carrying a box, and he placed it in my hands. Then he left, disappeared into the crowd. I brought it home, but unfortunately it wasn't much, just a box of rather dingy stationery. I thought maybe someone had written on the stationery in invisible ink so I ironed the sheets of paper and all those things you're supposed to do, but nothing happened. Nevertheless, I felt in that moment that I had somehow made contact with that person, that there was a kind of intimacy set up, and I felt something about the world in that offering, because that is what he gave me.

EW: Larry Weller has a moment like that, a moment of seeing the world clearly, when he visits a maze for the first time, the 1690 maze at Hampton Court in England.

CS: Yes, he has this experience, as I think people do in a maze. It's a very interesting environment where you are in a state of controlled panic. You know you're going to get out because a maze is designed with an exit, but it's not going to happen until you have worked through the pattern. And there is something, I suppose, transcendent about being both lost and found in a single moment.

EW: In an essay that your eldest daughter, Anne, wrote about you and your work a few years ago, she said, "My mother takes one foot off the ground, rarely both." Are there any instances of both?

CS: You know your children always see you differently than you see yourself. As a mother, I suppose, I had to stay pretty close to the earth for a number of years, but I've always been interested in speculative ideas, which work better in short fiction than in novels, which tend to be fairly naturalistic. But I like curious ideas and psychological phenomena. Maybe I'll get both feet off one of these days.

EW: In middle age, Larry starts to think about the nature of words and their tendency, as you put it, to "slip loose from their meanings." How does that work? Where do these words go?

CS: There's the famous case of the theologian Paul Tillich talking about this. He was staring at a carton of milk on the kitchen table and the word "milk" suddenly swam into incomprehension. I'm sure you've all had that experience, where words suddenly become meaningless symbols. Certain words have this quality of losing their sense for us. I'm interested in people changing and transforming. I've never believed — we used to be haunted by this as children — that our personalities are formed by the age of seven and we can never escape this inheritance. It seems to me that people are always changing, and changing quite dramatically, and that what changes them is access to language and the ability to expand their expression of themselves through language. So Larry Weller, a man with a somewhat limited education, realizes he doesn't have enough words, and if he's going to get any closer to that self of his, he's going to have to learn more words. And that is what this part of the book is about.

EW: Is it because the only way you can attain self-awareness is to have the vocabulary for it? You can't simply intuit somehow in a non-verbal way?

CS: Maybe you can, but I always see everything through the screen of language. I understand there's a part of our experience that leaks around the edges of language, and perhaps we have to appreciate that, too. But I think when we finally articulate something to ourselves, we have to articulate it in words.

EW: On a slightly different tack, one question that keeps coming up, whether in the charming book by Lynne Sharon Schwartz, *Ruined by Reading*, or implicitly almost everywhere else, is: why do we read novels? Apart from liking a good story, or the vicarious experience of getting into other people's lives, or gaining access to the interior of people's lives, what is it?

CS: Why do we read novels? It's a question I've been thinking about a good deal lately, because when you're writing a novel, sometimes you lose faith in that enterprise and you want to know why you yourself read novels. And I think we still live in a society that questions our right to dive into what is basically an illusion. I always think of what Nabokov said, that reality is the only word in the language that always requires a set of quotation marks around it. So this idea of illusion and reality is interesting. For a long time, I've felt that reading novels is not escape; it's a necessary enlargement of my life. I always think our lives are so sadly limited, even the most fortunate of us. We can only work at so many jobs, we can only live in so many places and experience so much. Through fiction we can undertake those journeys and yet remain at home and enormously expand our comprehension of the universe. As one of my characters — Judith Gill in *Small Ceremonies* — says, "My own life isn't enough for me."

EW: I think another reason is company. People who carry novels around want company.

CS: That's what Saint Augustine called "conversations with the absent." I think that's an interesting phrase because in those days, the fifth century, reading was done aloud — almost no one read silently — so it really was a conversation.

EW: Book clubs are very popular now. You not only occasionally speak at them, but you belong to one yourself. Why, since you read so much anyway?

CS: It's a way in our modern society for people to come together on a regular basis. There seems to be a human need to do that. It's like bridge clubs, I suppose; it doesn't really matter what we do, it's the coming together. Anyone who belongs to a book club will tell you this, that it forces you to read books that you might not otherwise pick up. And it seems to me that the first thing you want to do when you read a book that drives you to either anger or great pleasure is to talk about it, and so this seems like a perfectly natural expression to me, to be with other people who've actually travelled the same text that you have travelled. Of course, we talk about the book and then we talk about our own lives, but it's the book that provides a jumping-off point and topic for discussion. It's an enormous pleasure to me, and I don't like to ever miss my book club.

EW: And why do you think they've become almost exclusively female?

CS: I wonder about that too. I recently went to a mixed book club as a guest. I was interested to see if they would do what we do, which is to break off into private discussions of our mothers-in-law or whatever, and they did. I found it very reassuring.

EW: There's a piece in the latest *New Yorker* about new fiction, new anthologies of writing. They quote the editor of one of these, who, in trying to introduce the work, says a rather surprising thing: "the best writers reveal something about themselves that a smarter person would choose to hide." Does this ring true to you?

CS: Yes. This is a painful part about becoming a novelist. You think you're veiling everything under this illusion, but in fact you are revealing, both by commission and omission, what you don't even realize. I can give you a couple of examples of this. I recently had a letter from a dental hygienist in northern California. She happens to write a column for the national journal of dental hygienists, and she wanted to write a little about me. The reason was, she said, because there are so many teeth in my novels. And then she proceeded to quote, with page numbers, all the places I had mentioned teeth. She wanted to know why I had. I had really never noticed this drift toward dental hygiene. I wrote back that teeth are a part of life, an important part of life, you have to maintain them and use them and so on, but even to me that sounded inadequate. So now I have to subject myself to severe analysis and find out what it is.

An omission was also pointed out to me by a French journalist. She had read everything I've written, and she pointed out that there are no animals in my books. I was shocked. I did think, There is a dead parrot in one of my stories, but the fact is, I grew up in a household where my mother didn't let us have cats or dogs, and I married someone who is allergic to cats and dogs, and so animals haven't figured —

EW: *The Orange Fish* didn't count?

CS: That's only a picture of an orange fish. I thought of that. So you don't know, in a funny way, what you are revealing by these patterns in your work. It is interesting and it's also frightening how much we expose ourselves.

EW: At the end of your own review of Lucy Maud Montgomery's *Journals* in last week's *Globe and Mail*, you write about "the transcendent and healing possibility of art." Can you say what writing has meant in your own life?

CS: I think a lot about this business of art and who makes it and who gets to name the culture in our society. And what it means to make art. Without getting too pretentious about this, I think that the ability to take the words in my head and put them on paper has again and again rescued me from what I might think of as emotional bankruptcy. The fact that I can actually still do this has given me a sense of making something. The filmmaker Jean Renoir once described art this way: "art is making." It's a very nice definition, and it's exactly what I feel. Art isn't looking at something and appreciating; it is actually making. And I feel that this making that I have been privileged to do has given a centre to my life that I might not otherwise have. So healing, yes, in the sense that it's a place that I can go to; it's a refuge. It doesn't always work perfectly. And I know that when I have a good day that I'm going to be punished for it the next day. There are bad days, the days when everything you put on paper doesn't match that golden book in your head, but getting it as close as possible gives me a kind of pleasure that very few other things do.

EW: For those of us who can't write or make things, how do we address the emotional bankruptcy?

CS: I always think that everyone is creative in one way or another — I've never quite mastered this great dialogue about what is art and what is craft. I honestly think that to make a wonderful meal, for example, or to grow a fine lawn is a creative act that sustains us. Even the ability to tell a good story over the dinner table is a creative act; it gives pleasure to others and to ourselves. It is a making of something.

EW: The first line of your first novel, *Small Ceremonies*, is "Sunday night. And the thought strikes me that I ought to be happier than I am." The last line of your most recent novel, *Larry's Party*, is "Regrets only." [Beth is giving Larry a blanket invitation to a party at her house.] It's a lot better than Daisy Goodwill's final, unspoken words at the end of *The Stone Diaries*, "I am not at peace." I just wondered, do you have regrets? I know you were playing with that word.

CS: Of course, it's a common phrase that we all use on invitation cards, but it's an interesting one. If you think of it in the French way — they use the word "regret" in a more forceful way than we do.

I suppose I have some regrets. Now what would they be, and what would I be brave enough to say out loud? I never worked. I never had a job after I finished university. I regret that a little bit, that I had no period of economic independence, and I'm very glad that my own children did. They married later and had that experience. I don't regret that I didn't start writing earlier because I don't think I could have written earlier, I don't think that I had anything at all to write about. I didn't have a sense of structure or really any notion of how to use language. I think that came to me a little later than it did to most people. I don't regret the direction of my life.

Another thing is that you have to compromise with the history you're born into. I lived at a time when this was the path that middle-class girls took. Our lives were very predictable: we knew we were going to get married and have children, and we never thought about what was going to happen next. That was what we were handed. A few people rebelled against that, but most lived with the strictures that were given to them, like Daisy Goodwill.

I suppose I've been lucky in that I've found work that I love to do and that I hope to go on doing. I've been lucky in friendship and love and family, so I've found a place where I can be productive.

EW: You recently attended your forty-fifth high school reunion in Oak Park, Illinois. What was that like for you?

CS: There were moments of confusion. As you know, I always feel that we live our lives in chapters, and that one chapter ends pretty clearly before the next one begins. But I felt last weekend that I was standing in two chapters at the same time. All that adolescent ungainliness came back to me so that I was walking across a flat surface and my right foot tripped over my left foot. I thought that my body knew something was wrong with that moment.

Why do we want to go back to the past? I asked myself why I would do this. Because I value these friendships for one thing, but I think going back to the past awakens old and very interesting questions. One thing I've never written about, and perhaps I can file this under regrets, is my own childhood, my own growing up. Of course, we all know that children are not interested in childhood. When we are children, we just want to get out of it. But it's when you get older that you really look back and try to understand how you saw things for the first time, the freshness of those early impressions, and try to open that place again. So all of those things were reasons for going back in time, and I suppose there's such a thing as just feasting on nostalgia. It's a meal.

"Throttled by Astonishment"
DRESSING UP FOR THE CARNIVAL
ONSTAGE AT THE INTERNATIONAL FESTIVAL OF AUTHORS
TORONTO, OCTOBER 1999

EW: Your new book of short stories, which is coming out this spring, is called *Dressing Up for the Carnival*, and it's full of whimsy, whether it's a harp flying out of an office window, or a grandmother who invents a muff for a steering wheel, or women who are dying for love but don't. It's playful, even a bit wacky. For instance, when the weathermen go on strike and there's no more weather.

CS: You may think these things are all fanciful, but, in fact, most of them have some basis in truth. I do remember one summer in France there was a meteorologists' strike, so the next question — and I suppose every writer does this — you ask yourself is, What are the possibilities here? And so this came out of a real story. The story about the harp came from a story that my daughter told me. She was invited to a cocktail party in Vancouver, the annual gathering of the accountants' association, and they were very late in getting started. They had a harp there for the cocktail hour, which, unfortunately, went on far too long. And when dinner finally was ready, the master of ceremonies stepped up, and he strummed on the harp to get everyone's attention. The harp fell over and out the window. I just had to write a story about that from the point of view of someone who was passing on the street. So these are all highly naturalistic stories, really.

EW: In another story, you have the Earthquake Man and the Rainfall Woman working hard to understand the topography of the real, and I thought, Well, that's what you're doing, working hard to understand the topography of the real. Tell me about this.

CS: Sometimes I don't think I know what is reality and what lies outside that reality. But what I have seen in fiction, certainly some South American fiction that we have all had some exposure to, is that the area of the real is getting larger. What we admit to our world of reality is gathering a little more space. And, of course, we see this in the scientific world. Things that we thought were impossible are shown to be otherwise and actually do occur. Possibility is all around us, and it lies in the future.

I just heard a wonderful story about Alexander Graham Bell who, shortly after he invented the telephone, made a speech in which he said, "People here in this audience will think that I am being a foolish visionary, but I predict that in the future every city will have a telephone."

I was asked recently to write a millennium essay, as, I think, has every writer in the world. This puts you in the very serious position of having to predict, and probably being very wrong about, the future. But I was writing about the family, and that is something I felt fairly safe about. Because we are vertebrates, because we are mammals, the family has to continue, I think, at least for another hundred years. After that, who knows?

EW: The title story, "Dressing Up for the Carnival," looks at a number of different characters who project themselves into different roles. Small acts — pushing a baby carriage, buying flowers, carrying a mango — allow them to see themselves differently. Why do they do this? What are they looking for?

CS: I think we all dress up every day of our lives. We have to get up in the morning, and we have to reinvent ourselves, and for this we need a little costume help. The story came to me when one of my daughters was at York University and was living a fairly poor student life. Occasionally, she would be asked out for dinner, and she would buy flowers in the morning so she could carry them with her all day before she actually presented them in the evening, and so people would look at her and say, "Oh, there's a young girl with flowers! She's expected somewhere. She's going to have an evening, a festivity." And then someone else told me about a woman who took a bag lunch to work every day, but she always carried it in an old violin case. And nowadays — and you've all seen this, it's the joke of the decade — people with their cellphones, talking as they're going down the street. They have a certain mannerism, a certain telephone walk that they assume, and it seems to me they're saying to us, "You see, I'm not really lonely. I've really connected to someone. You only think I'm alone." So the story is about different people who carry something or wear something that they have spent a little time thinking about, actually, and it's their defence against the world, and, heaven knows, we all need to defend ourselves a little bit, even if it's only with a few brushes of mascara.

EW: Defend ourselves from what?

CS: From being misunderstood, from being scorned, from being laughed at, from being thought foolish, from not fitting in. The everyday frights of the world are enormous, and we have to keep them at bay somehow.

EW: And when you say that every day we have to reinvent ourselves, I know what the words mean, but what does this really mean? Of course, we have to put clothes on and think for a moment about —

CS: There is such a thing as a core to the human personality, and I think we do carry that with us, more or less, but I guess

I see people as being fairly fragile. I think most of us lose the sense of that core once every day or once every hour for a minute or two. We lose a sense of faith in our arrangements — and I think this happens particularly early in the day, when we're waking up and dealing with our dreams and getting ourselves wide awake — and we have to remind ourselves of who we are and re-establish ourselves and give ourselves a little jolt of courage.

EW: I was thinking about how, in *Larry's Party*, your most recent novel, Larry often feels like a fraud who will be unmasked at any moment, and when he accidentally takes a jacket that's better than his, he can't really wear it because he feels he doesn't deserve it, it doesn't fit who he is. Do you have that sense?

CS: Oh, all the time. And certainly, my most extreme case was on Thursday night, here at the [International Festival of Authors] tribute to me. I felt an imposter. And women, of course, are much more susceptible to these kinds of feelings, that other people see more there than they know is there. But perhaps we all have those feelings of basic unworthiness, which occasionally are shored up by one happenstance or another.

EW: By the end of the evening, were you shored up?

CS: Until the next morning, when I woke up.

EW: You begin your collection with the story "Dressing Up for the Carnival," and you end with a story called "Dressing Down," about a man who starts a naturist, or nudist, camp. What interested you in that?

CS: I thought it might be a nice framing device, and I had always wanted to write about a nudist camp.

EW: Why?

CS: Well, I was walking one day on a beach with my daughter Sara. One minute we were on a regular beach with people in bathing suits, and the next minute we were on another kind of beach altogether, a nudist beach. Sarah thought it was all right as long as they were just lying around, but when they were leaping around playing volleyball, this was going a bit too far. And, of course, I have to confess — I was a little younger then — we joined them in the ritual because you feel suddenly terribly overdressed. But I can remember how curiously disappointed I was to come across this scene because everyone had the same basic form — some were larger than others, some were taller — but really, pretty well the same clefts and hollows and mounds, and there was something rather reductive about this. Our clothes really do bring something individual to us. I had read an article about someone whose parents were naturists, as they're called — a lovely word — and how embarrassed she was by this when her parents would drag her off to their events. It is a curious way to see your parents and other adults and children. I just wanted to think about it a little bit, so that's what the story came out of.

EW: It's a bit like the writer Joan Brady, whose parents were nudists. She fell in love with a friend of her mother's, and one of his chief attractions was, she said, that he wore clothes.

In this story, the wife of the man who starts the naturist camp likes wearing lots of clothes, and, in fact, her whole house is layered with fabrics and carpets and curtains. You were creating a foil here. But what were you wanting to do with that topic?

CS: In the story, her husband asks her if she will surrender her body coverings for one month a year and join him at the naturist camp, and she does, out of love for him, but always with resentment that he is asking her to be something that she cannot comfortably be. But she does it anyway. I suppose I was talking about the exchange of bargains that any marriage involves, and this is a bargain that they made.

EW: At the end of the story "Dressing Down," the narrator has come to the truth that "Nature's substance is gnarled and knotted in its grain so that no absolutely straight thing can come of it." What was that about?

CS: I think I was saying that it may seem easy to elect for yourself a very different way of being, but, in fact, it's not easy because you're surrendering so many things at one time. These arrangements of ours are far too complicated to be reduced to simply saying, "Let's take our clothes off and live this way for a while." It involves our sense of self. We violate not just our sense of modesty but our sense of who we are, our sense of how we perceive other people. I think it affects all the senses and sends us terribly off balance when we take these kinds of steps.

EW: Hearing you talk about sense of self and who we are reminds me that this is something that comes up a lot in your work: what makes a life, who people are. Why is that such a preoccupation of yours?

CS: I think it's a preoccupation for everybody, really. People used to use the expression "getting in touch with my feelings, getting in touch with myself," and I always wondered what on earth they meant by this. Did they mean the self you were yesterday or the day before yesterday? The self never seems to me to be a static thing. It's ever-changing and literally changing from moment to moment, as the rest of the world bounces off us. I'm not quite sure of the stability of the self. It's like thinking about what Canada is and what it isn't. You know how we used to talk about defining our country, and finally I think everyone gave up. Our identity is that we don't have an identity, or we don't need to seek an identity. I think the same applies to knowing ourselves, that we can never quite know ourselves. We really can't predict how we're going to respond to future events. We may be able to accept momentous events with a shrug, or we may simply cave in. I'm not sure we can predict our behaviour, our response to what confronts us.

EW: When you say that, are you thinking particularly of what has confronted you in these last years?

CS: Yes, I am thinking of that. People always say about novelists that their fiction darkens as they get older, and I think that this is perfectly natural; we know, by a certain age, that terrible things do happen to people. People suddenly distrust what they have so laboriously constructed. And confronted with a serious illness, I had no idea how I would have predicted my own response, so it has been a surprise. It has made me a more frightened human being but, at the same time, more thoughtful, I suppose, and more thankful for certain parts of my life that have been lived without this kind of confrontation.

EW: I want to talk more about that in a moment, but when you say that fiction writers typically get darker in their books — you mentioned this when we talked about *The Stone Diaries* — then you turned around and wrote *Larry's Party*, which, although it has a lot of different tones and colours, is actually quite an optimistic book.

CS: Yes. It may be more optimistic than I intended. But after I wrote *The Stone Diaries*, which was a sad book, I actually worried when people told me they had bought the book for their grandmothers, because I thought it delivered bad news to women of a certain age, that perhaps their lives had not had as much meaning as they had meant to bring to it. I didn't necessarily want to write a happier book. I wanted to write a book about someone in that period of life where the major decisions are being made about how life is going to work out. Larry, you remember, was between twenty-six and forty-six in *Larry's Party*. I wanted to deal with this more active part of life. Being at a time in your life where you're making choices, I think, is very different from being where Daisy Goodwill is.

I had a curious sense writing *The Stone Diaries*, if I can go back to that for a moment, because I wanted to write about a woman's whole life, from birth until her nineties, and I wanted a chapter for each decade. My thought was to cut in about every ten years to see what was happening to her. But I got to the middle of the book and she was already old. I had thought, Here's your life, and here's this little old age bit at the end, so that was a surprise to me, to find out how long someone spends being old. I had to think what I could do with that so it wouldn't just slide straight downhill.

EW: About a year ago, you were diagnosed with breast cancer, and it's like one of those cracks in the surface that you sometimes write about or, in this case, maybe a chasm, revealing a frightening fragility in our lives. Can you talk about it?

CS: Yes, I can. Of course, it was a great surprise. I had very naively thought all these years that I was not the breast cancer type — whatever that is — and it turned out that I was. First of all, there's a feeling of unreality. It took me a good month, maybe a little longer, to actually accept that this was the reality, that this was happening. I couldn't turn it back, I couldn't dismiss what had invaded my body. Then I did accept it because there's really nothing else to do.

Then you get in touch with other people who are going through this, which is enormously helpful, and I understood, for the first time, why people with different diseases form these associations: they need the experience of other people so that they don't feel alone in their sorrow.

I suppose I was surprised by how good people were to me, how people looked after me and took over so much of what

I had formerly dealt with by myself. There was a lot of giving over, and that implies some loss of self-sovereignty in a sense, but it was something that I certainly had to do for a while.

There's an up-and-down period of going through treatments and hearing success stories, and then you read obituaries in the newspaper and hear the stories that are not . . . And then you become, I think, quite philosophical about it in the end, and that's where I am now. I feel that I don't know the future. I can't plan for the future, as I once thought I could, and that's fine. It's fine. I can plan a month ahead, and that feels fairly comfortable at the moment.

EW: When you talked about it recently, you said you felt that you inhabited a "new self, a stranger who remained throttled by astonishment."

CS: Yes, I was. I could hardly breathe at first for the surprise of it, the shock of it. But then I just learned to — people talk about living with cancer, and there is a way to live with it. I think you have to avoid reading all those little statistical tables. I needed to find distractions, and that's what I did during the early period. I had intended to watch some television, which I never do, but I ended up not doing that at all. I ended up reading novels — not that I have found novels an escape. I've never thought of fiction in terms of escape, but as a way of enlarging my own experience. So with the help of many friends — and certainly with your help — I just settled into a program of reading.

EW: What did you look for in those books?

CS: I looked for novels that were a little different from what I usually read, novels that were more cheerful and had more narrative movement to them. I don't usually require much narrative movement in the novels that I read. And characters — I always think of Darwin when I say this because Darwin is famous for doing his science work in the morning and then, in the afternoon, having someone in the family read a novel to him. They would ask, "What kind of novel? What should we read you?" And he always said, "It doesn't matter as long as there's someone in the novel I can truly love." So I wanted to read novels about people I could love and feel a sense of kinship with. And I wanted to read funny novels — actually, you found me some good funny novels. The fact is, I don't think we have enough funny novels. Life is very rich in comedy, but for some reason, not a lot of it gets into our serious fiction.

EW: What are some of the books you read then?

CS: Quite a lot of British fiction. I read Ian McEwan's books. Did I read them in the right order? No. You told me, Eleanor, to read them in the right order, and I read them backwards. I read an Englishwoman, Barbara Trapido. I loved her books; they had humour, which I was looking for. They also had great depth of feeling. She's good at writing about young people and tragic events and somehow pulling all this together. I've enjoyed meeting her at this festival too. I read some biography. I'm always happy to read biography because, of course, the novels that I like and like to write are rather unplotted. My favourite plot is the arc of the human life, so biography was a good thing for me to read at that time.

EW: Why do you think humour is missing from serious literature? Do you think it's considered trite by publishers?

CS: Yes, probably. The no-longer-quotable Woody Allen once said that comic novelists always have to sit at the children's table. I think it's true. I used to like a writer called Peter De Vries. His work was wonderfully funny but quite dark too. The trouble is that he often used slapstick humour, which I sometimes love, but the kind of humour I prefer, of course, is ironic humour, where there's something confronting the characters that cannot be dealt with in any other way except as part of the comic fabric of the world. I have written a few novels, not so much about academic life, but that touch on academic life, and anyone who's spent any time in a university knows that this is very rich material for humour.

EW: You said people encouraged you to keep a cancer journal.

CS: Yes, everyone encouraged me to keep a cancer journal. I think they thought, Oh, well, she's a writer, she's having this experience — but I had a lot of trouble with it. I just didn't feel like doing it. I had no interest. I had to drag myself off sometimes just to do a sentence a day, but I was glad that I did in the end because it helped me keep track of what I was going through, the peaks and troughs, the false hope and then something going wrong, and then more optimism and then the dashing of that. You begin to see this as a kind of natural rhythm in your life, and it helps you, I think, to accept it.

I had trouble with it at first because, for some reason — I don't know why — I was trying to make it amusing, trying to make it funny, like "Erma Bombeck Gets Cancer." And then I just realized one day, I don't have to do this. This is a life-and-death illness. I don't have to make this amusing. It's for *me*, anyway, this journal.

EW: How do you think this experience — this part of your life — has or will affect your own writing, your more literary writing?

CS: I'm not sure. I haven't done that much new writing, although I did do one short story in which a woman has breast cancer. I think it's rather incidental to this story. I'm just more conscious of mortality. I've lived a life where I haven't really spent a lot of time thinking about mortality. I haven't lost anyone close to me at an early age, for example. A lot of the bad things of life have not touched me. I've been extremely fortunate. Now I have to think about these things much more directly. And if I'm not thinking of it actively, I'm sure there is what a friend of mine calls the "cancer eye": whatever you look at, you see with an eye to its possible diminishment or its increased worth. It seemed to me, when I first became ill, that I didn't want to rush out and write one last novel. I didn't think there was much point to it. The world didn't need another novel. Of course, I always think this when I go to enormous bookstores and see mounds of books. Who needs another book, anyway? Who do we think we're fooling?

EW: But usually you feel more driven to write.

CS: Yes. And I think that will come back, that I will feel the need to invest more of myself in my writing.

EW: You've talked about being concerned about — this is how you put it — "the unsettling self-absorption" that cancer had led you into. How did you escape that?

CS: I don't know that I have. One of the things that has worried me more than anything else is self-absorption. Every muscle that twitches, every little pain you feel — you're always listening to your inner music and testing yourself against the healthy people in the world. I worried about this, that it would make me too self-absorbed. Part of the joy of my life has been reaching out and having people around. They say writers aren't sociable, but they are. They are terribly sociable beings.

EW: And you've talked about your "desperate curiosity," as you once said.

CS: Yes, and I didn't want to lose that. I think the worry is diminishing now because I'm feeling a little stronger, and I'm living in a different place this year. I'm having new experiences every day. I'm getting out of this terrible introspection.

EW: You're writing a short book, a monograph about Jane Austen, who's always been one of your favourites.

CS: I didn't choose Jane Austen. The publishers Lipper/Viking are doing a series of twenty short biographies, and they're asking mostly novelists to do these books. They asked me if I would do Jane Austen. In a way, it's a good match, because she's been a hobby of mine over the years. I have done a couple of academic papers on her and have always been interested and very curious about how her novels actually work. It's very hard to see what makes them work because there's a lot that's not *in* the novels, a lot that she chooses to leave out, and so what is left is interesting. You know that the characters are going to get married in the end, and you can always pick them out. You can pick out who the husband is going to be because he's the one who reads books, and you know this right from the beginning. Jane Austen would never pair up her heroines with un-bookish men. But even knowing this, even knowing the conclusion, you still turn the pages because they're dramatic. And in my later readings, not when I was a teenager — I just read them as love stories then — I came to see the humour in them. Now I see the tragedy as well. At different ages, I've seen different things. So she's an interesting but very frustrating biographical subject.

EW: What are you learning from focusing on her now?

CS: Of course, I'm always interested in the shape of a human life, and her life was a short one. She died in 1817, at forty-one. She did so much of her writing when she was in her late teens and early twenties. It's astonishing how at least three of those novels were pretty well in focus by the time she was twenty-one. And then she had a long silence before she went back and, in her final years, wrote the last three novels. It was an odd writing life. I'm learning that she was a curious woman, that she was regarded as an eccentric woman in her time, and I believe that.

She was also someone, I think, who suffered. We've all felt, reading Jane Austen, that there's a psychic wound there, but what is it, and where did it come from? Some of the biographers have pointed to the fact that, very early, she was banished from home. Her mother was a member of the gentry, and most women of her time sent their children out to a wet nurse, but her mother was unusual in that she fed her babies at home herself. Then she sent them out. She didn't want toddlers around the house. So her babies — and there were eight of them — were just removed from the intimacy of the mother connection and were farmed out to a foster home for, we think, two or three years. No one knows exactly. Nowadays, we would consider that to be a rather abrupt cessation of any kind of nurture. She was also sent away again when she was seven to a terrible boarding school, where she almost died of illness. She was sent away once again to school, and then she was dispatched to Bath. She was always being sent away. She had no control. She had no money, no power. She was at the service of others all her life. And I think that's where her psychic wound lay.

And she also knew from the beginning — I'm convinced she knew — how good she was as a writer. She knew, but she had to pretend in a demure way that she was only someone who scribbled. I don't think she was allowed to say, "I'm a genius," although she was, and that, I think, probably did her a lot of harm. So that's some of what I'm learning about her.

But, unfortunately, she lives in the unreachable past. There's no photograph of her, not even one. There's no voice recording. There's no diary. There are letters but not a lot of them because many were burned after she died. And the letters are little, girlish performance pieces, on the whole. They don't go very far. She wasn't a great letter writer, and she certainly wasn't an intimate letter writer. So, how do you get there? The only way, really, has been through the novels, and I'm not sure that's always fair. I'm always concerned when people mistake my novels for my autobiography, because they're not.

EW: Your own life, and certainly your professional life, took a very different shape from, say, Jane Austen's in terms of when you did most of your writing. You grew up in Oak Park, Illinois, near Chicago, which was also the hometown of Ernest Hemingway.

CS: Yes, Ernest Hemingway left and never went back. It was a restricted suburb; there were no blacks, no Asians — no one who looked very different at all from us. I didn't catch on for a long time that there just wasn't enough there. There were excellent schools and good friends and a secure family, but I think that I knew I would leave.

Now, I do go back. I'm not like Ernest Hemingway. They even named the library after Hemingway, and he still wouldn't go back. But I have, and it's been interesting. It's an entirely different place now. It's a racially mixed community. It's very progressive, a wonderful place. But those days — 1940s and fifties — were perhaps a sterile period in our history, although it never felt that way to me.

I left when I was eighteen to go to university.

EW: Going back to childhood for a moment, you mentioned last year that you've never written about your own childhood. Why is that?

CS: I suppose because it hasn't seemed very interesting to me. Looking back on it now, I see all kinds of ruptures on what I thought was a smooth surface, and so that might be interesting to look back on and write about. I see that life now quite differently. I knew people who didn't have two parents. Not everyone lived in a nice, roomy house. There were problems, all kinds of problems, that somehow weren't acknowledged, but they existed, and I might go back and look at that kind of Midwestern upbringing of that period.

Most mothers stayed home, and my mother did for a while. She wore an apron and made pickles and did all those things that women did. But then she went back to teaching; it was very unusual to have a working mother. There weren't many. Most of my friends' mothers were at home, so that made us a little different.

EW: You started writing poems and plays and essays even when you were still in primary school. Did you fantasize a life for yourself as a writer?

CS: I did, but it was like wanting to be a movie star. It seemed impossible, yet I used to say that I was going to be a poet when I grew up. I had no idea what that meant. But I was lavishly praised for the execrable poetry I wrote — I can't tell you how bad it was. Sometimes I think that's why I became a writer, because I really couldn't do anything else very well. My teachers encouraged me and my parents encouraged me. I always carried around in my bag the sonnet I was working on at that particular moment. I was a literary girl, every school has one of those girls, and that was what I grew into, but it took me a long time to actually think that I could be a writer — I had never met a writer. We didn't have writers-in-school programs or anything like that, so they seemed exotic creatures. It would have been useful to have met some writers and to see that they're just ordinary people.

The American poet John Crowe Ransom came and gave a talk in our town to a women's group, and one of my teachers bundled a few of us literary types into a taxi and took us to see this man, an enormous, statuesque personage, talking about poetry, and he was a real poet. I remember that that was a very encouraging thing for me to see.

EW: You've written about fledgling artists of one sort or another, especially women, who come to recognize who they are and can be. Do you know how that happened with you, when you much later, as you say, came to see that you could be an artist?

CS: I think it came through a love of language. I felt that very early in my life: the importance of language, more than the substance. And I suppose I still feel, when I'm writing, that I'm more interested in language, the sound, than I am in what Nabokov calls the "aboutness" of fiction. The two have to go together, the style and substance, but I'm interested in the way the language comes out and goes onto the page, how you can give it voice or make it dance somehow or make it mean more than it did in your previous version: I love to try to get more out of it than I did on my first attempt.

EW: You said recently that novels are about finding our true home, that maybe we've lost our sense of it, or it's been mis-assigned in the first place. Is this one of those perennial searches, the Odyssean search for home, or does one actually find it?

CS: I don't think one always finds it, but more and more, I do think that novels — and I don't want to use the word "literary" novels but novels that have a weight in our culture — are about this search. And when I say "home," I mean the place where we are enabled, where we can be at ease, and, of course, where we can be creative, where we're free to be creative, where we're at peace with other people: this is our true home. The search is a sort of longing for belonging, I think, and people don't always get there in their lives, but I think that most of us are trying to find that place. John Cheever used to talk about how he pictured himself sitting under an apple tree, at peace, with a book in his hand, of course. He never quite got there, to that particular tableau.

EW: Have *you* got there? Or are you still searching for this place of belonging?

CS: I've done quite a bit of it in my life, not as much as many people did, but in the 1960s and seventies, people used to change jobs and move all over the place. I did move around, but I was always with my family. The family was moving with me, and they constituted a sense of home. And, yes, I think more and more that I have reached that place of being allowed to do what I want to do. It's a very curious freedom. You'd think everyone should have that freedom. But I wanted to write books, and I was allowed to write books. A great indulgence: I was able to do just that. I've had support. I haven't had to write a particular kind of book for any particular kind of market. I've been able to write exactly what I've wanted to write, so I suppose that is a way of finding your home.

EW: You once said that, of all your characters, it was Jack, the historian at the centre of your novel *Happenstance*, who was your favourite character. You've written more books and more characters since then. Do you have a favourite book of your own or a favourite character of your own now?

CS: I still like Jack very much, and I identify with him because he's someone who elected the stance of the outsider, looking rather than doing. He's a historian, and that's what historians do, I think. It's a posture that I have felt comfortable in. I'm not really a doer. I'm someone who watches other people do. So I still identify with him.

My favourite book, I have to say, is *Swann*. When I wrote that book, I was reading a lot of postmodern criticism, which can be very damaging to a writer, but at the same time, it had this effect: it made me realize how accommodating the novel form is. I had written four quite traditional novels, and suddenly it seemed to me that the novel could be much more elastic, and it could contain more. It seemed like a big, baggy thing that I could put anything into, and I did. I worried a little bit about whether this book would be published, of course. You always have to think about that. But, for some reason, I didn't care when I was writing that book. I felt that I could make a structure that was very different from the structure of my other novels, or of any novel that I'd ever read. I could do something quite different. There's a film script at the end of this novel, which a few people had trouble with, and I can remember the publisher saying, "Oh, couldn't you recast that? Isn't there something you could do?" But I was also filled with a lot of courage at that time in my life, and I said, "No, it's going to stay here. This is the way I want it to work." The novel doesn't work perfectly. I had an idea in mind of these two gears going around. One was a big gear, and it was the mystery of how art gets made, how people of ordinary breadth can make works of art, and I've never been able to figure that out. And then there's this little, tiny mystery going around, which is the mystery of the book: the disappearing manuscripts and the theft and so on — a kind of Tinkertoy mystery, it seems. And I wanted them to fit perfectly together. They don't quite do it. But I just loved the energy that was flowing through me when I wrote that book, so I remember it as a period of great happiness.

Letters, 1999 - 2001

London
21 November 1999

Dear Eleanor,

Tea at the Ritz was a bust. My editor (she is James Salter's daughter) hadn't made reservations, so we were swept over to a table by the door. The moment we sat down there was a bomb alert and everyone was asked to leave the hotel. We had checked our coats, but left them, ran around the block to Caviar House where we each had a "spoon" and two tiny pancakes and were rudely treated. The glimpse I had of the Ritz looked beautiful, however.

Don was in Manchester doing interviews and I was seeing my three old mates from our years there in the early sixties — we had a heavenly time, extraordinarily nostalgic.

Marjorie [Anderson] will be delighted to get your piece [for *Dropped Threads*]. I think there is only Keith Fulton's to come now, and Marjorie is going to give her a call and prod — she's been very busy with teaching. It is all coming together, except for one piece that we may not be able to use, a mother-daughter piece which we thought would add "texture."

I'm feeling not bad (have forgotten what good feels like, and all the gradations in between). Don and I did a V&A tour of Pimlico yesterday and enjoyed every minute, though it was terribly cold. We started out in Lord Linley's wood products shop where they sell beautiful things for astronomical prices. Two hundred dollars for a pencil cup — that's one of the affordable items. We enjoyed the other people on the tour and all ended up having tea at our guide's flat.

Rhombus hopes to film *The Stone Diaries* next summer. I've seen the script which needs just tweekings, or is that tweaking? Yes. One of them will be here tomorrow to discuss details.

Poor Jane Austen is not getting enough attention. Discipline is needed, definitely.

I'm almost done with the Coetzee [*Disgrace*] and admire the way he moves it along. Much discussion of lust/desire and how men shouldn't have to apologize for it — a little confusing philosophically. By the way, I have never met a single person who's read him. Nevertheless, this one is on the bestseller list here.

Is life rich and full? [A refrain I coined.] I'm about to make a marvellous lunch — I've made the most appalling meals lately.

much love, carol

Victoria, B.C.
25 January 2001

Dear Eleanor,

I've read the James Wood piece on the Atlas biography [of Saul Bellow]. I thought the first part was sheer brilliance and the last part — where he identifies the narrative direction, all through memory — very sharp. It was the middle section that "gave me pause." The "So what" part, where he says Bellow only damaged the lives of ten people (count them on the fingers of 2 hands, etc) and it was worth ten little lives to have the great novels. Well, now. I'm not so sure. How many lives are you allowed to smash in the name of art? Even

great art. Thank you so much for sending this. Makes me realize I
don't look at a great span of periodicals.

  Jane Austen, the bio, has a mistake in it (probably more than one).
Her aunt was accused of stealing the lace from a Bath shop, not a
London shop, as I have it. A small point, but noticed at once by my
friend Joan Austen-Leigh. The worst part is that I knew it was Bath.
I think I am happier writing fiction.

  much love, c

"A Gentle Satirist"

JANE AUSTEN

CAROL'S HOME, VICTORIA, MARCH 2001

EW: You've been interested in Jane Austen for a long time. What first attracted you to her?

CS: Austen was the first author I read who wrote about intelligent women, and when I was a young woman, I was looking for those kinds of books. Austen was how far back I had to go.

EW: When you first read her, was there a specific novel that you recall?

CS: Yes. I first read her as a teenager, actually, and it was very different reading. I read the love stories; they were romances to me. Probably *Pride and Prejudice* was the first one, but I remember that, once I started, I read them all. It was at the same age that I was reading Russian novels, so I suppose that was my idea of what novels were.

EW: How do you think she's influenced you? The very last sentence of your book about her, the very last sentence of the acknowledgments is "My debt to Jane Austen herself is incalculable."

CS: Of course, aside from inventing the contemporary psychological novel, she was a woman writing, and all the other great
novelists that I was studying at school — Dickens, the Russians
— none of these were women, so that was another thing. She
does something that can teach any novelist, I think, something
about the craft: she knows how to set up a scene and bring
it along quite quickly. I think people are often surprised how
readable these books are. After seeing the movie versions, those
people went to the books expecting something dense and slow
and dull and class-ridden, but, in fact, she moves her scenes
along at high speed, and they are self-contained, full of conversation, full of the kinds of people that we might know, full
of the kinds of problems that we might ourselves acknowledge.
I think all those things made me feel that I could maybe write
a novel.

EW: When we spoke about Jane Austen before, you said there
wasn't much to go on for a biographer: no photos, no record-
ings of her voice, no diaries. Much of her correspondence had
been destroyed. And yet you do somehow manage to piece
together a picture of who Jane Austen might have been. How
did you get there?

CS: What I did was this: I put everything on the bulletin board.
I put the criticism up there. I put the other biographies there.
I put up her letters, the ones we have. And then, of course, I
put the novels up and read everything as if it were one great
organism. And out of that came an image, my image, of what
this woman was like, and I felt more and more that she was
a woman who was trapped in the particular class structure of
her day. She was trapped in a historical time in which women,
unless they married — and she did not marry — were not
offered a life of their own. They didn't claim their own lives
and weren't allowed to make their own plans. She was, I think,
extremely isolated. She never travelled. She never went to
France. She never went to Scotland. She visited briefly just a

few counties in England. That was the extent of her travel. It was a very limited life.

EW: Let's look at Jane Austen's early life, her family life, for a moment. She was born on December 16, 1775, in Steventon, a small village in Hampshire. What do we know of her parents?

CS: Her parents were of the lesser gentry, her father lesser than her mother. Her father was the rector at Steventon, so he was an ordained clergyman, a very handsome fellow from what we know and, I think, quite a good father. At least, he encouraged all his children in whatever direction their lives took, and he certainly encouraged Jane in her literary writings. He was also a country gentleman. He played that role. He ran a small boarding school in the family house. They had four or five young boys boarding along with the big Austen family themselves, eight children.

EW: What did it mean to be a country gentleman of the lesser gentry?

CS: He was involved in owning land and in agriculture, and he went to local balls. The family was not as wealthy as some of their neighbours were, but because they were often better educated than their neighbours, they were accepted as acquaintances, and the neighbours played a big part in Jane Austen's life, taking a great deal of interest in the Austen children. The children went back and forth between the various families in a very congenial way.

EW: Was it surprising that he would encourage his daughter in her writing?

CS: I suppose it is a bit surprising. We think of the clergy at that time as being rather disapproving of novels, but Mr.

Austen was not in the least disapproving. He loved novels. The whole family loved novels. They used a lending library in Basingstoke, but they also bought novels, which were the family entertainment. They read trash along with the good stuff. They weren't very discerning, and indeed those classifications of literature hadn't been established in the late eighteenth century. Novels were novels, and they read what came along with great enjoyment. So when his daughter Jane began writing just for the family's entertainment, I think he was absolutely delighted, and so was her mother.

Now, her mother was someone who wrote comic verse, some of which has survived; you can still read it and see in it her wit at work. We don't know much about her mother. We know that she was an enormously busy woman, running this household: her own family, ten of them, the students who were boarding at their house, laundry, meals. There were servants, of course, but some of this had to be supervised. They had some poultry and kept cows. So I think that she would have been so preoccupied that the children were left very much to their own devices a good deal of the time. This was probably a good thing for an imaginative young child who would grow up to be a novelist — to have time on her hands, time to spend as she wanted, time to be unsupervised.

EW: You draw attention to the fact that, unlike most infants of that time, Jane Austen was nursed by her own mother, but then she was sent out to be looked after by another family until she'd reached, I think, the age of reason. What effect do you think that had on her?

CS: I don't know, but I can only imagine it would be devastating to be taken from her mother's breast and boarded out in a nearby farmhouse, where she, as well as her siblings, were put until they could walk and, I suppose, make themselves understood. We don't know how long they were boarded out. We know that the family visited them almost every day.

The parents would visit the children, so they weren't simply wrenched from home completely. But I would guess that the environment was very, very different and that would have to have an effect on any child.

EW: How would you describe Jane Austen's relationship with her mother?

CS: People often talk about Jane Austen having a difficult relationship with her mother, and there is a kind of myth — it's very hard to pin this down — that her mother was a difficult woman; that is, she was someone who required a lot of attention herself, who made a great deal of her small illnesses, and that there was tension between her and her daughter Jane. We only get hints of this in Jane Austen's letters to her sister. It's almost as though they communicate in a kind of code about their mother and the demands that she made. But there's not a lot of hard evidence that her mother was this difficult, neurotic, demanding woman, so it's hard to know exactly what the relationship was like. There's an example that I sometimes think about when Jane Austen was at the beginning of her last and what would be fatal illness. Her mother was occupying the sofa, so Jane lined up three chairs and made that her sofa. That's where she would lie down during the day, and somehow you would think her mother would not have allowed this and would have wanted to see her daughter on the sofa, thinking about her children first. Or maybe Jane Austen was participating in some kind of a martyrdom, showing up her mother. We don't know. It's funny about families, which is what she writes about, and a family is ultimately covered by curtains. We don't know how they operate or what goes on inside families.

EW: And you point out that her novels are not necessarily about marriage and getting married and who you marry, but about the relationships between parents and children.

CS: She often touches on neglectful parents, parents who neglect a particular child, and that is the child that she chooses
to champion. Think of Elizabeth Bennet, not her mother's favourite, although certainly her father's favourite — Elizabeth
triumphs over her mother. There's not much Darwinism in
Jane Austen's psychology. These brilliant children come from
dull parents, and sometimes you have to ask yourself, how on
earth does this happen?

EW: Jane's own environment in her early years at Steventon
seems so full of stimulating activity, not only with the older
brothers who were at home but with the young boys at her
father's school. They put on homemade theatricals. What effect
do you think that had on young Jane Austen?

CS: I think she had a marvellous childhood, as long as she was
at home. She was, of course, boarded out as an infant, and later
sent away twice to school, not very good schools, along with
her sister, Cassandra. She didn't thrive in these schools and
had a great deal of scorn for schoolmistresses and the kind of
accomplishments they were taught. She was a child who was
happy at home, where her family understood her. Probably
a rather odd child — this is how I see her. But we all know
how precocious children are tolerated within their own family
group, though maybe not so well tolerated outside it. I think
she had a childhood in which she was free to read. I think she
probably read everything she wanted. I don't think there was
anyone looking over her shoulder and censoring her choices.

EW: What kinds of things would she have been reading?

CS: She was reading Dr. Johnson when she was still a very
young child, for example. She loved the poet George Crabbe,
and she writes a great deal about him later. She loved the poets.
Of course, we know she read *Tom Jones* and loved it, that she

read Samuel Richardson and was very much taken into that hugely romantic and melodramatic world.

EW: It seems like she started writing at a very young age. How did she come to write?

CS: She started writing early, and it wasn't private scribbling at all. This was writing that she would then read to the family. She wrote a series of short — and I do mean short — novels. The chapters might only be a page. She wrote a little history of England, a comical history of England. Everything was at the level of farce, and everything was intended to deliberately shock her parents. These writings, this juvenile writing, is full of violence, neglectful parents, rapes and abductions and sexual innuendo. Coming from the pen of a clergyman's daughter, this is all fairly shocking, but somehow one gets the impression that her parents weren't terribly shocked, that Jane knew they understood that she was striving for a reaction, and they reacted. They were interested in what she was producing. It is amazing.

EW: How seriously do you think Jane Austen herself took these very early writings?

CS: I think she took them seriously because she kept them, she guarded them all her life, and she even went back and amended them at times. We also know that she took them seriously because they got better. The really shocking and violent parts of them became more subtle. Her dialogue became more manageable, more realistic. She was moving toward the kinds of novels that she would eventually write.

EW: Jane Austen's most intimate relationship was with her sister, Cassandra. What was she like?

CS: Cassandra was two years older than Jane Austen, and I imagine that the Austens were quite delighted to have had a second daughter as a playmate for their first. They were extremely close. When they were both at home, they spent the day together. When they were separated, they wrote to each other, as far as we know, every day, or very frequently, at least. As the younger sister, there is always the sense that Jane was somewhat infantilized by Cassandra, who was always considered a woman of enormous virtue and correctness and one who had a great deal of influence over her younger sister, a younger sister who was — we can see this in the letters — often trying to placate Cassandra, to appease her, to please her with funny stories in her letters. And I think there's a sense in which the closeness of that relationship can be questioned, that some of it, anyway, was perhaps damaging to Jane Austen, not in her writing so much as in the person she became.

EW: In what way?

CS: She was always dependent on her sister's good opinion. When *Mansfield Park* was published, it got a very quiet reception. Of course, she eagerly sought the opinion of her siblings and friends. Cassandra was rather harsh about that book. I think we can read in her letters the sense of injury that Jane Austen felt.

EW: In terms of her dependence, they shared a bedroom even when they didn't have to. Was that out of habit do you think, or were they still that close? This is when they were in their thirties and early forties.

CS: Yes. I can well imagine that they shared a bedroom all their lives out of habit, that this was always the way it had been. It felt comfortable. This is how they went to sleep at night, picking up each other's thoughts, picking up each other's sentences probably. They were very much like a married couple in that sense.

EW: But Jane Austen herself wanted to get married; we know that.

CS: We know she did. For years, she kept on going to balls, becoming more and more discouraged by her lack of partners. At the age of twenty-seven, she did accept a marriage proposal from Harris Bigg-Wither, a wealthy young man she knew, who was a few years younger than she was. She accepted in the evening and changed her mind by morning, but we don't know what thoughts went through her head deciding against this marriage. Clearly, she didn't love him. He was not a bookish man, and all her heroes were men who read. She was probably fond of him but not willing to share a married life with him.

EW: Do you think the loss of her first beau, Tom Lefroy, was a tragedy for her?

CS: It's often thought of as a tragedy in Jane Austen's life, this meeting with a young man who seemed absolutely perfect and fulfilled all her definitions of what a young husband should be. He was dashing, intelligent. He loved to read — very important — and they had a long discussion about *Tom Jones*, which was a rather risqué topic. But the marriage was not thought a very good idea by his family, because Jane Austen could not bring money into it. This was, of course, always the problem, that there was nothing she could bring to a marriage other than herself, so that kept suitors at a distance. Is this a tragedy in her life? All that matters is that she thought of it as a tragedy — and I think she did, yes, I think she did — an opportunity missed to form a happy life with someone she admired.

EW: You quote a very poignant letter that she wrote to Cassandra, in which she suggests that she expects a proposal. One can just imagine the devastation and disappointment when it didn't come.

CS: Yes. And humiliation, of course, because she had confided in Cassandra. And the haste with which this young man was whisked away from the neighbourhood must have injured her, too. That she was not quite up to his standard — yes, I think it was a time of humiliation, heartbreak. She was very young. I think she rebounded from that, to a certain extent, but probably looked back fondly all her life to that moment of being in love, of expecting the world to open for her.

EW: The theme of marriage comes up frequently in Jane Austen's writing; it seems to have been an important aspect of her world. Another of Jane Austen's biographers, Claire Tomalin, says that a woman needed a wealthy father or husband because if you were a woman, you could only hope to be creative or imaginative if you were rich. How do you think Jane Austen saw this?

CS: I think Jane Austen saw marriage as the only chance a woman had to make a home of her own. She actually uses that phrase a number of times, "making a home of one's own." Think of Charlotte Lucas in *Pride and Prejudice* accepting Mr. Collins, who has already been turned down by two other women. Why would she accept a man who is so comically inept? Because he could give her a home of her own, and that was worth accepting at Charlotte's age.

Having a home of your own meant that you could leave the dominion of your father's house and set up your own. You were still in for a lot of dependence, as you had been as a girl. You certainly were not going to be completely independent. It's simply a *degree* of independence, more than Jane Austen ever realized — the poor woman was chaperoned right to the end of her life. Whereas a married woman could be unchaperoned, could make an independent life to a certain extent, as you suggest, a life of the imagination.

I think she did what she could do with what she was left. She knew fairly early that she would not marry, I think, after the debacle of the one-night engagement. I think she knew by age twenty-seven that she was not going to find a husband, that no one would come along and rescue her from her parents. And neither would she be able to rescue her parents from their poverty. That was another thing she hoped to do by making a good marriage, to provide for her family. Her novels became the place where she put her energy.

EW: So it was within the framework of the novels that she could give the smart, bright women the marriages that they needed?

CS: Yes. All these marriages were marriages of love. All her heroines married for love.

EW: The money came along with it, though.

CS: The money came along with it. Emma is the only one who actually had money of her own. Fanny Price, from *Mansfield Park*, had no money and no family at all to support her; although she's not an orphan, her status is that of an orphan who is taken in by rich relatives to be raised.

EW: When you read more about what you refer to as the debacle of her accepting, at twenty-seven, a marriage proposal and then rejecting it the next morning, this occurred after she had written in one of her own novels that by the time you're twenty-seven, you're unlikely to find love or appreciation or anything.

CS: Yes. After the age of twenty-seven, one has lost one's bloom. That's a word she uses a lot — that word that means a wonderful, healthy skin, that first skin of youth. It seems a bit young to us today. We might think that if a woman hasn't married at thirty-seven or even forty-seven, maybe she won't marry. But for Jane Austen, it was twenty-seven, and I think she felt pretty much on the shelf by that age.

EW: When you read about that instance though, do you think she should have accepted? It's funny how we get involved in the same way that we read novels; we read about people's lives, and we think, you could have had money, you could have gotten away from your parents.

CS: And she could have. Harris Bigg-Wither was a very wealthy man who would inherit Manydown Park, but I think she felt a kind of repugnance for him, which made the situation impossible. I have nothing that informs me of that, but she was extraordinarily fastidious, and I suspect that she simply couldn't enter into a loveless marriage with him.

EW: And we do know that she did believe in love in the sense that there's a letter to a niece advising her to marry for love.

CS: Yes. It is very curious. I always think it's curious that all her heroines marry for love, but around her, she must have seen all sorts of people who were marrying for completely different reasons. These novels are a projection of a kind — they do have a fairy-tale quality — of finding true love. And we know who will come together because Jane Austen goes to great pains to sketch out what these men are like, and they're often clergymen. But as I said, they're men who possess tact with women, who respect women, and who read, which is very important for Jane Austen.

EW: Her nephew wrote that she may never have met even her own intellectual equal. In that sense, these novels would reflect her ideal that women find intellectual equals.

CS: Yes, I think the women do find intellectual equals. And, of course, the books are filled with other people who do have intellectual powers and who are able to converse brilliantly. So she was building her own universe, I think, with the nib of her pen.

EW: But do you see them as romances or satires or both?

CS: As an adult reader, I don't see them as romances. I know many people do, and I understand what they mean when they say that they are projections of an idealized world. I don't think the worlds that she makes are particularly idealized. I think there are a lot of muddy roads in these books and a lot of hardship and illness. There's much that's idealized. She does understand satire, and we always have trouble understanding how she could have been a satirist as a child, but that's when her satiric powers were at their most brutal. I think she came to be much more of a gentle satirist. We all know that you can't satirize the powerless, and I think she understood that fairly early in her life; we don't get rustic servants in her novels or foolish working people. People are made fools of only when they're pretentious or a bit pathetic, like Miss Bates in *Emma*, but, otherwise, she doesn't make fun of people that she might easily have made fun of — never once.

EW: What do you think might have become of Jane Austen as a writer if she had married?

CS: Oh, this is a wonderful question, and I often ask myself this. As a mother who is a novelist, I have more than one perspective. Being a parent, of course, makes you a witness to the development of personality, and I think that's one thing that mothers who write can bring to their writing. But time is a problem for anyone who has ever had even one child. The organized time to sit — Jane Austen always called it "composing," not "writing," which is a wonderful word. Even without children, she had to steal time from her household tasks. Of course, the family had servants, but there were many things that the women of the house did themselves, and she would have had to find that precious time for her composing. Would her imagination have stood up to the realities of motherhood? I can only guess that she might have written a little but perhaps not have fulfilled her major achievement: the redesigning of the novel. The novels are very different. Each one can be considered an experiment with reality. If she had had children and a busy family life, she might not have had that time to concentrate, to bring about the kinds of experiments she wanted to bring about.

EW: I'd like to look at Jane Austen's writing itself for a moment. The novel in the late eighteenth century was still, as you pointed out, a relatively new form.

CS: We know some of the novels that she read. Fanny Burney, of course, had been writing novels, but they were epistolary novels and had gone out of fashion. Jane Austen actually tried her hand at an epistolary novel, but it was not the kind of thing she was good at. So when she found the kind of novel that she wanted to write, which was, as she has famously said, about three or four families in a village, she would work at them, fitting those families together. She was often tempted to change that formula, and toward the end of her life when she wrote *Sanditon*, which is the novel that she never finished, we do see the novel going in a different direction, much more modern in its sensibility, much more accepting of change in the world. But the novels that she wrote were primarily about the world she knew: remote village life in England intermingled with scenes of London and Bath — the two urban areas she was familiar with.

EW: You call it "brave and original" of Austen to look at the microcosmic world of people's everyday lives. How was this different from the work of other novelists?

CS: I think the novels she read were about extreme acts, extreme human possibilities, entanglements and violence, with complete historical backgrounds inserted. She didn't do that. She alluded to historical occasions, to changes in her society, but this was all background for the people that she invented, the people who actually exchange views, who have relationships with each other, who betroth and promise and mingle their lives.

EW: When *Sense and Sensibility* and *Pride and Prejudice* were finally published, they did very well. What do you think accounted for their popularity at the time?

CS: I think when you look at other novels that were being written then, hers are just better written, better conceived, more rooted in psychological necessity. They have characters one can love. I think this is a very important part of the appeal of Jane Austen's work. She knew that we had to love — or, at least, in the cases of Emma and Fanny — had to feel some affection for these characters in the situations where they found themselves.

EW: In terms of the likeability of her heroines, Austen was a little concerned about the character of Fanny Price in *Mansfield Park*. You suggest that readers wish she might just once recognize her priggishness. Tell me about Fanny. What kind of a person is she?

CS: Fanny is really a feeble version of Elizabeth Bennet, I suppose. She is feeble in every way: in her actions and in her health, as a matter of fact. She is entirely passive. She has a great deal of moral rectitude. She never makes a false step, and she never admits, not even once, how priggish she really is. If there had been one admission, one confession, I think it would have rescued Fanny for a lot of readers, but, in fact, she insists on a kind of self-righteousness that one can only despise.

Unless we think of her — and I do think of her this way — as someone who is, of all the Jane Austen heroines, the least entitled. She comes from a terrible home. Her father was a rough-talking drinker. Her mother was a slattern who preferred the boys to the girls in the family. She had no place in that world, she with her very fine moral nuances. And so she was plucked from that world and put into Mansfield Park, which was the place where she was educated in her sensibility. She's in a curious position — and this is the great irony of that novel — because Fanny Price saves Mansfield Park, but Mansfield Park has already saved her from her life in Portsmouth. So we have this cycle with its built-in tensions, which is deeply ironic, even though I think that Jane Austen tried to write that novel without her usual irony.

EW: Why was Jane Austen so attached to Fanny Price? She called her "my Fanny." Or was it *Mansfield Park*, the novel itself, that she was attached to?

CS: I think that Austen felt that her earlier novels were not serious enough, and there's a kind of self-punishment going on with *Mansfield Park*, in which she writes something that she believes really has moral force in the world. She takes Fanny very, very seriously, and she hopes the reader will too. But her other characters, with their moral dilemmas, are actually much more attractive to readers than Fanny is ever able to be.

EW: Did Jane Austen have a favourite amongst her heroines?

CS: I don't know. But I do know that when the first published copy of *Pride and Prejudice* was delivered to Chawton Cottage, she writes to her sister that her own darling child has arrived. And I think she loved Elizabeth Bennet, the person that Jane Austen would like to have been if she had had a chance to play a role in the world. She would have had the bravery, the intelligence, the sparkle, even the sexuality, of Elizabeth Bennet.

EW: Do you have a favourite Jane Austen heroine?

CS: I'm very fond of Anne Elliot in *Persuasion*, which we

haven't talked about. Anne is the oldest of the Austen heroines. She's in her late twenties and has lost her bloom, as Jane Austen tells us quite plainly. She has ruptured her life by turning a young man down seven years earlier, but she meets up with him again, and this is the story about how they re-knit their relationship. She doesn't have the pomposity of Fanny Price. She's a thinking woman; she's articulate in her speech; she's willing to enter into arguments about the role of women. Now, Jane Austen felt she was a little bit too good to be true. She was a little disappointed in the way Anne Elliot worked out. But I think she is a heroine for our times too. Her self-assurance is winning. And her ability to say that she had made a mistake, to confess that, I think, makes her admirable in our eyes.

EW: Jane Austen died in 1817, when she was forty-one, and there are various speculations about her illness. Can you talk about her last days?

CS: She was sick for about six months before she finally died — "in failing health," as they said. She had a number of symptoms that we know about, one of which was the up-and-downness of her illness. She would feel very well one day and not very well the next, almost right up to the time she died in the summer of 1817. This is consistent with certain forms of cancer. People didn't talk much about cancer in those days and certainly weren't able to diagnose it always, but I think this is the most probable cause of her death.

EW: You say that "what is known of Jane Austen's life will never be enough to account for the greatness of her novels." In your moments of wishful thinking, what else would you like to have? What kinds of things would you like to have access to that would shed more light on her greatness?

CS: One always dreams about coming across a diary, but people didn't write that kind of confessional diary in those days. That's much more of a contemporary activity. But it would be interesting to have more letters, for example. We don't have many letters, and we know that some of them were destroyed after her death, letters that reflected, I suppose, badly on her. The letters that we do have show her often to be quite vicious, and so we can only imagine that what was destroyed was much more of the same, only intensified, but it would be good to have them. We could understand her better. I suppose we wish — and this is an academic comment to make and I'll probably withdraw it immediately — that she'd written more about her writing, about her literary thoughts, about the novels she read. I wish she'd written book reviews and offered up her philosophical theories about the novel and talked about novel-making, how she actually made those novels. It would be wonderful to have a little more of that.

EW: You've often been compared to Jane Austen for, as one critic put it, your "elegantly plotted, deceptively domestic novels," and because you've written so much about women. Do you feel a kinship?

CS: I don't think my novels are anything like Jane Austen's novels. You know how people are always comparing women to Katherine Mansfield, for example, when they're nothing like Katherine Mansfield. It's a kind of shorthand, just saying that they're women, and that this is the area they've chosen to write about. So I suppose I don't feel much kinship. But I think that she has much to teach a novelist by the way in which she dives into her stories and the way in which she sets up a scene. This is something novelists need to know very early in their writing life: that novels are composed of scenes, and scenes have to be furnished, and you have to stay in the scene. I think this is something she does well. Now, she's not a great describer of meals or clothes or the kind of surface details that interest me very much. She's much more of a dramatic writer than a describing writer, and I suppose one would wish for more of that too. I think that she had great skill with dialogue and later with monologue — her monologues are wonderful; there's one in *Emma* that's just hilarious and breathtaking. She figured that out herself — there weren't other novelists doing that at the time — and she knew she was good at it.

EW: Did you learn something new about writing from this biography?

CS: I suppose I learned that we can't really look to a writer's novels to decipher a writer's life. I don't feel that the novels helped me a great deal, not nearly as much as the letters, for example. It's a different voice. Jane Austen's voice in the novels is different from her voice in the letters. We feel we're further from her, I think. And I don't feel that writing biographies by relying on the fictional production helps us very much in understanding one's life. There's a real separation between oneself and what one writes.

EW: And does knowing more about the self enhance the experience of reading the novels?

CS: I think it does, actually. We don't like to admit that very often, but I think the more we know about a writer, the more we understand how the novel was put together and why and what it means. And maybe we don't need to know this. Maybe we don't need to know anything about the writer. Maybe it's better for us to enter blindly into the reading of novels, but, of course, I am always curious about the person behind the voice, behind the writing hand.

Letters, 2001 - 2002

Victoria
29 January 2001

Dear Eleanor,

I heard last night after all, because it took us all that hour to drive
in the dark and rain to Sidney. We thought it was a great interview all
through [Art Spiegelman], but I especially loved and latched on to his
idea of neo-sincerity as the only stance for those who had read *MAD*
magazine. It seemed to chime with my notion of willed innocence in
a world that has witnessed such horrors in our century — which I'm
trying to incorporate in the novel. (The "novel" she says, what novel?
It is now a husk.) Didn't you love what he said at the end of the
interview, about not knowing before where it would go, something
like that. He was so beautifully and sleekly nonpretentious. And so
grateful for all you understood and had read. We also heard the story
[by Grace Paley], which took our breath(s) away. Could anyone doubt
the authority of that voice!

How sad about Lorna Sage [author of *Bad Blood*] and what a loss.
I have the feeling of wanting to write to someone, but who?

Am off to chemo right this minute.

love, c

Victoria
25 March 2002

Eleanor — Geoffrey [Wall, biographer of Flaubert] was the most
endearing and engaging of guests. He laughed so beautifully, paused
so perfectly, seemed to be stopping to scratch his head — so that he
could put into words his instincts. I was in love, standing over the
ironing board.

much love, c

"Ideas of Goodness"
UNLESS
CAROL'S HOME, VICTORIA, JANUARY 2002

EW: *Unless* is an unusual title for a novel. In your book, you describe it as "the worry word of the English language," "the little subjunctive mineral that you carry along in your pocket crease. It's always there, or else not there." Why *Unless*?

CS: The idea for the title came to me from a philosophy professor whose office was next to mine at the University of Manitoba. He was going off to give a lecture one day, in a very fine mood, and he said, "I'm going to give my favourite lecture of the year." So I said, "What is it?" And he said, "It's called 'Unless.'" And that's when I found out that "unless" is a term that's used in logic. There's even a sign for it, which is a big U, lying on its side. I used it in the book, in somewhat the same way, as a means of getting into a narrative and turning it over, revealing an alternate reality. So this idea of fiction and "reality" is something that has always interested me and certainly did while I was writing this book.

EW: What is this distinction between fiction and "reality" about?

147

CS: The idea that bad things can happen to us, that trouble can come to us and disrupt us. But underneath it, unless somehow it was prevented from coming, unless something is done — there is always this alternative way for events to proceed.

EW: In reality?

CS: In reality, no. We can't really flip that button very much. In fiction we can. I think of fiction as the other side of reality, often as just another side. I'm sure you've seen silk embroidery which is beautifully finished on both sides. I think of reality and fiction as something like that.

EW: But in fiction, presumably, the fiction that you write yourself, you can control everything that happens.

CS: Yes. The fiction writer, one supposes, can control the story to a certain extent, within believable limits, and make something happen, something to interrupt the period of unhappiness. Or I suppose one can choose to bring more unhappiness, another storm of grief into people's lives.

EW: I want to ask you more about this funny word "unless," these odd pieces of language, these little chips of grammar, as you put it, because there are all kinds of words like this, and you use them as chapter titles, a whole catalogue of them: once, next, following, hardly, since. And you say these are everyday words that we take for granted, words that don't seem to bear much weight. But you put weight on them here.

CS: Yes. I love these words. They're words that grammarians and lexicographers have trouble with, defining exactly these little chips of the language that we use, which really situate us in a more-or-less particular position. They're often adverbs, not the usual adverbs but adverbs of position. And I find them resonant, I find them poetic and full of echoes, so I liked using them as chapter heads.

EW: The usual adverbs modify verbs, like "he walked slowly." But each time, I would read a chapter title and think, Is that an adverb? What is that? Whether, ever, as. They situate us in what way?

CS: They situate us in space, they situate us in a narrative, they call upon other parts of the language. I think they should be kept in a little box all by themselves over in a corner of the tool box, and when you need one of them, you just reach for it.

EW: And when do you need one?

CS: Like "however," when you're just about to tell another story, another narrative, or "since," and particularly the word "unless."

EW: What is it about that word?

CS: I like to think that it's a hopeful word, that it can draw into being a whole other set of possibilities to work with, instead of the regular nuts and bolts that are in the tool box.

EW: "Unless" is a worry word, as you put it, and this is a novel with a lot of worry in it; its preoccupations run deep. As your central character, Reta Winters, says at the start, "It happens that I'm going through a period of great unhappiness and loss just now." Why take on unhappiness as a subject?

CS: I suppose it's just a big piece of life. I don't know what our happiness/unhappiness quotient would look like. I suppose we're unhappy as often as we are happy.

EW: It's so central to our experience, and so mysterious some-times too.

CS: Yes, yes. Why we should be overcome by grief. And in the case of this novel, there is a cause: Reta's nineteen-year-old daughter has dropped out of university, dropped out of life, and has become a street person, has distanced herself from the family. This is the grief: the estrangement from a child, which I have always believed must be the most difficult thing to come to understand in your life.

EW: You obviously wanted to start with a very unhappy situa-tion. Why is that? I can't think of another novel of yours that begins with unhappiness. Your characters might encounter it or fear it, but to start from that place . . .

CS: Yes, that is unusual, I have to admit. If I think of my other novels, one begins in the reality of the moment, and then either happiness or unhappiness comes, and then the result of that comes next. But this one starts in the midst of unhappiness, and I'm not quite sure why. Maybe I was deeply unhappy myself when I started this book, and perhaps it just came out of that.

EW: Happiness is, of course, famously elusive, both to know and to understand. As your narrator observes, "I'm supposed to be Reta Winters, that sunny woman, but something happened when my back was turned." *Happenstance*, the title of one of your early novels, and happiness are closely related in their original meanings of luck and fortune. Can you talk about how they're connected for you?

CS: Happiness and happenstance. Generally, I have tended to write about people who find their way to happiness, who understand what happiness is and that we can make it part of our lives. But life brings us other images, and every day we run into people who have been shattered by an event or a series of events — something that has removed their ability to control their lives and their happiness, where they are, in fact, helpless but have to keep on going somehow. Well, how do we keep going? I suppose this novel is about how one woman, Reta Winters, keeps going through this period of unhappiness. She finds other things to preoccupy her. I think all the strategies of the unhappy are brought forward. She's writing a novel. In the beginning, she's writing a novel about happy people who become unhappy. This is, I suppose, the swing of the pendulum that every one of us knows and understands.

EW: You were saying that, when you began this novel, you may yourself have been in a place of unhappiness, yet you chose to inhabit a character who was also unhappy. Was that useful for you? Better than inhabiting your own unhappiness, in an odd way?

CS: Yes, I think — and I won't make this a general rule, because I can think of a hundred exceptions right now — that people, or novelists, have an easier time of it if they assign their particular feelings to one of their characters rather than carry these themselves. Also, in some way, to change the quality or the cause of the unhappiness from one thing to another so that you're not forever writing your own autobiography, which is the last thing that most of us want to do.

EW: Happiness is something your characters have reflected on before, though not quite in this devastating way. For instance, the narrator here, Reta, is planning her next novel, and she's already written the first sentence. She says, "Alicia was not as happy as she deserved to be." Now, this echoes the first sentences of your first novel, *Small Ceremonies*, which is "Sunday night. And the thought strikes me that I ought to be happier than I am." Tell me about this. What's going on here?

CS: I'm always thinking about this, and I think other people are thinking about it too: how happy are we right at this moment in time? I might reply, "I'm perfectly happy, except that I didn't get the job I wanted, and one of my oldest friends is ill." So I can't be totally happy. I can't have that one hundred per cent feeling of sunrays coming out of me, like in a cartoon. There's always something worrying away at us, something that is going to reverse the situation and make us unhappy instead of happy. But most people don't ever ask this question.

EW: They ask the more generic "How are you?"

CS: They say, "How are you?" "How are you doing?" "How do you do?" But we very rarely reply with "I'm about seventy-three per cent."

EW: Happy. This idea that you deserve to be happy or you ought to be happy — were you deliberately echoing your own work?

CS: Yes, I think I was. Yes, I was deliberately echoing my own opening sentence.

EW: And do you think there is a sense that we feel we deserve to be happy or ought to be happy?

CS: Yes, I think we deserve to be happy. I think people deserve a reasonable amount of happiness, of things going well with them. And why not? We live in a world that's full of blessings for us, a world full of beautiful landscapes, a world of flowers, of good food, culture. All the resources, art, are at our disposal. We should be happy. We should be made happy. Unfortunately, we don't yet know how to make ourselves completely happy. Somehow, we start out thinking something is going to make us happy, and it fails us.

EW: We aren't the agents of our own happiness.

CS: We're not really the agents of our happiness, no. I think we can be, but it doesn't happen very often.

EW: We can be? Are you able to do that for yourself?

CS: I think when we say to people, "Oh, come on. Pull up your socks. This isn't as bad as it looks, and you're grieving about nothing." — I think we try to tell people this, to no avail. We continue to decide for ourselves how large grief is going to be in our lives; we assign its proportions.

EW: You think we have control over that?

CS: I suppose it's in our nature really, which is not quite the same thing as having control, is it? But I think people have been, as they say, turned around by various therapies or medications or maybe just one good thing happening to them, like winning a raffle.

EW: And your little unless word is one of those . . .

CS: Yes. Unless I win the lottery next week. Yes.

EW: Reta's grief revolves around, as you say, her eldest daughter, Norah, who at nineteen suddenly abandons a promising future — university, a boyfriend — for a life on the street in pursuit of "goodness." She's "gone to goodness" — "a goodness," as Reta puts it, "in which silence is wiser than words and inaction better than action." Goodness is one of the novel's preoccupations. What does it mean?

CS: For me, it's the main preoccupation of the book. I've been interested in the idea of goodness for a number of years. I certainly believe in it. I'm like those people who talk about modern art, and they say, "I don't understand it but I know it when I see it." I feel I know goodness when I see it, but I

have a very hard time defining what it is. I have felt myself
the recipient of a great deal of goodness in my life, maybe
particularly in recent years, of other people's goodness: people
writing me long letters, people I don't even know, or helping
me in ways that I haven't even thought to ask for. So I believe
in a flow of goodness in the world. I don't know why people
are good. I've certainly read about the altruism gene but think
it goes beyond that.

When I heard that the aid workers were back in Afghanistan
so soon after the smoke cleared, I had to think that there's a
kind of goodness in operation there. These are young people
risking their lives. And you think sometimes, too, about the
naive people who send anonymous gifts of money to flood
victims and to people across the world. Who are these people?
What motivates them? And why do they do it? I think people
are happier when they perform acts of goodness. That's all I
can say. They're happier doing something. And the amount
of evil in the world that we read about all the time lately is,
I believe, relatively insignificant. It's a wonder that so many
people are good, not that so many people are evil.

EW: Do you know why the idea of what it means to be good
has come to preoccupy you more recently?

CS: I think, sometimes, that we think of goodness as doing
nothing. The idea of "do no harm," "make no enemies," "don't
defile the planet" — it's become an act of standing still and
doing nothing. And this is the path that Norah, the daughter in
the novel, takes. She doesn't know how to be great, and she's
not allowed to be great, but she can be good; that is, she can
do no harm.

EW: And do you believe that? What you described earlier was
people doing positive good rather than neutral "no harm."

CS: No, I don't believe that standing by is an act of goodness, though I suppose it could be.

EW: Reta writes letters that she may or may not send —

CS: Yes, Reta writes letters all the time, venting her rage, mainly her feminist rage, and I think it's something we all do. We don't really write these letters — we think them. We think about letters to the editor that we could write to set those people straight. And sometimes you get a letter from someone who says, "I feel as though I've written you three or four letters, but here I am, at last." They've written to you in their head well in advance. It's a way, I think, that Reta copes with what she thinks is the underlying cause of Norah's frustration, which is her inability to enter what we call the male world. She's shut out simply because she's a woman.

EW: Just to go back to goodness for a second: one of Reta's letters is to the author of a book called *The Goodness Gap*, where goodness is seen as a kind of problem solving, requiring creative solutions. Now, this seemed to me to be a spoof on *The Ingenuity Gap*, this year's Governor General's non-fiction winner by Thomas Homer-Dixon. What were you getting at?

CS: Oh, I think I just borrowed the title. I never got far enough into the book to feel that I was capable of spoofing it. But it was a book in which there is very little presence of women. It's a male view of the world, and of problem solving in that male world.

EW: So this was another instance of Reta's rage against the exclusion of women?

CS: Yes, the casual disregard of women, which is really worse, in a way, than the more visible forms of aggression against women.

EW: You're saying that this is Reta's overarching view of what's wrong with Norah. Is it yours?

CS: I think that Norah undergoes a very violent act, just as she witnesses a violent act, which causes a kind of post-traumatic shock, as people describe it. I don't think anything's simple. People don't break down for one reason. They break down for a dozen reasons, or a dozen reasons swim into the same orbit at the same time, unluckily for the person. By the age of nineteen or twenty, you're beginning to know what your place is in the world, and I think you can see, as a young woman, that your place is not going to be assured. It's probably not going to be allowed.

EW: So Reta's indignation is your own.

CS: Reta's indignation is projected onto Norah's, very largely. I think it's a fragile age — eighteen, nineteen, twenty — where you're looking around. You're supposed to be grown up. You're supposed to be mature. You're supposed to be on your own. And you look around, and all the doors are closed to you, or a great many of them are.

EW: One of the most startling things about *Unless* is the fierceness of it. When you come across scenes of Reta and her friends at their weekly coffee gatherings, it's easy to think, for all the consciousness-raising that went on back in the sixties, that things haven't really changed that much. What do you think?

CS: Things haven't really changed that much. A few big acts of legislation have made more areas of work open for women, but just a year ago, I heard [the British literary critic] George Steiner say that he didn't believe there were any women writers of the twentieth century. That gave me pause. What does he mean? He says in the nineteenth century there were one or two women, but he doesn't see women as a force in literature.

Particularly in literature, I think, women have been given very minor roles, not taken seriously.

EW: Even today?

CS: Even today.

EW: You've described this as your most overtly feminist book to date. Did that surprise you?

CS: Yes, it did. For some reason, I felt I could say some of the things I was thinking, and I was thinking about some things that I hadn't thought through before. So I came to a place where I felt I could say these things.

I was the woman in the audience, by the way, who asked George Steiner the question, What about women writers? So maybe I took the reply more personally than if I'd just listened to someone else pose that question.

EW: One of the women's topics of discussion is rage itself, not feminist rage but a sense of violence and unpredictability in the world around them, like being struck by lightning or having planes crash into your house. Is this something that you yourself feel, this unpredictability?

CS: Yes, I do. We all lived through September 11, so we all know that the unpredictable is, in a sense, almost predictable, that this cycle in our history, if we just go back far enough — this cycle of fanaticism and tyranny and then rage released — is something we can almost expect will happen.

EW: Reta and her friends discuss a horrifying incident in the news about a veiled woman, probably Muslim, setting fire to herself on a busy corner in downtown Toronto, and she died nameless and faceless. Did something like this really happen?

CS: Something like this often happens in the world. If you pick up the paper, the idea of self-immolation or the recent suicide bombings, yes, it's part of our world history at the moment.

EW: It also seems like a perfect metaphor for the kind of powerlessness and voicelessness that Reta is observing, this haunting image of self-obliteration. So, *are* you surprised to be writing such a feminist book right now?

CS: When a novelist sits down to write a novel, there are a few things you have to establish, and if you're going to write a traditional novel with some coherence to it, one is whether your main character is going to be male or female. It's very tempting for women writers to write about a man because, Jane Austen aside, a male character has more moral weight. Whether you work for this *gravitas* in the novel or not, it's simply assumed. I think this tells us something about the weight that we attach to the male presence and male thinking and male writing.

Now Jane Austen is a little different, and maybe this is why I've always been an enthusiastic reader of her work. Her women are at the moral centre of the novels, though they use traditional female wiles to get themselves power, which is male-controlled, of course. But they are able to manage affairs by their own quick wits and charm.

EW: Why do you think you had the confidence to write this now? Or have you felt yourself becoming increasingly radicalized with the years?

CS: Yes, I think I have become increasingly radical. I was slow to start. I was slow waking up. In the seventies, for example, I never went to any consciousness-raising events. I would have gone — happily — if someone had invited me. I didn't catch up to the women's movement until the eighties, but I've been a part of it in a small way ever since. I spend a lot of my time thinking about it and a lot of my time counting, counting how many men are mentioned, say, on the front page of a newspaper as against how many women, counting men in photographs of some new committee, counting members of Parliament. We all know that the number of women has slipped downward. So I seem to be bean counting all the time. It's a great burden. It's an irritation. I wish I didn't have to do it, but I'm too conscious of it not to think about it.

EW: I remember your telling me once about an issue of the *New Yorker* where there wasn't a single woman contributor. Did you actually write a letter?

CS: I did. But all I got was a polite reply that my letter was being processed. Not even one of the poets — they always have two poems — was a woman. I don't know who notices these things. I know a few of my friends do because we talk about it. But I have to think that they didn't notice at the *New Yorker* office because they would have put in a little explanation or something for this state of affairs.

EW: "The Men's Issue."

CS: "The Men's Issue," yes.

EW: Your character Reta translates the work of a celebrated French scholar, Danielle Westerman, an eighty-five-year-old woman, a Holocaust survivor, a feminist intellectual, an original thinker. She's something of a model and a mentor to Reta as well as a friend. Can you talk about their relationship, the role that she plays in Reta's life?

CS: Yes. She's the mentor that I never had. I always wished I had a mentor. I was thinking about this the other day. At the college I went to, Hanover, there was a single, older woman, a Shakespeare scholar. We thought she was a bit of a nut. We used to make fun of her and do imitations of her. And here she was, in the middle of Indiana, trying to be a Shakespeare scholar. I regret that terribly because maybe I could have had women models if I'd known where to look for them. As with many women of my generation, I didn't have role models.

EW: So you created this one for Reta.

CS: Yes, and I like Danielle very much; she's absolutely a created character. I don't know anyone quite like her.

EW: I was thinking that, in a way, she seems to embody European suffering and experience versus a kind of North American innocence and ease. Was that at play as well?

CS: Of course. I read Simone de Beauvoir with great energy for about a year once, and I think there's something of her in that portrait.

EW: Something else that happens in *Unless*: there's an incident that appears in slightly different form in your short story collection *Dressing Up for the Carnival*. In the story called "The Scarf," the Reta character, on a promotional tour, shops for a special gift for her daughter. It's one of those rare experiences where, with perseverance, she actually finds the perfect item, exactly as she imagined it. Why did you want to revisit that story here?

CS: Oh, I didn't want to revisit the story so much as I wanted to shake the voice from the story and write a novel. I wanted to write a novel in the first person, which I haven't done for many, many years, not since my first two novels, and I was trying to find a voice that wasn't too ironic. I thought, Maybe I could go back and use the voice from that story and somehow incorporate the story into the novel. So that's how it happened. It just gave me a little bit of a head start to have a few things in place.

EW: Even within that story, there are two things that seem possibly at odds. On the one hand, making someone happy doesn't matter, says the narrative voice, because, with the scarf, it may or may not go to the person she had in mind. But then she decides, it doesn't matter, as long as you make someone happy. And then within the same paragraph almost, she says, "Not one of us" — that is, the person she bought the scarf for, the person she ends up giving the scarf to, the women in her life, her mother, her mother-in-law — "Not one of us was going to get what we wanted." Are those two things at odds in a way?

CS: Perhaps at odds. The idea of goodness, of trying to make people happy, of doing things for people that we love, trying to make them happy. But getting what we want requires being able to articulate that sentence, "I want" — what? Women have not been able to make those kinds of demands on society. What women tend to say is, "This is good for the family," "This is good for all of us." But what I want is something that is forbidden — the very idea of the "I" wanting.

EW: Early on Reta says, "I want, I want, I want. I don't actually say these last words. I just thump along on their short, stubbed feet, their little, dead, declarative syllables."

CS: Women in the twenty-first century haven't had much practice at expressing our wants. I think we can hardly do it as women. It's only recently we've known what we can do as far as work in the world goes, how narrow the options were for our mothers or even for us as young women. There really wasn't a lot offered to us and certainly not an invitation to want more.

EW: There's something about the "short, stubbed feet" — it's a kind of a force just in that sentence — the "little, dead, declarative syllables."

CS: I suppose it's the not being able to complete that sentence, not knowing what we want or deserve. It always comes down to that, of course, for women: what we deserve and what's good enough for us.

EW: I don't think motherhood has ever been central in quite this way in your fiction, and, in fact, since your own children have grown, you haven't featured children much. Ever since *Swann*, kids haven't been big in the books. You've said — this was in the context of Jane Austen — that "being a parent makes you witness to the development of a personality." What have you seen, what have you learned?

CS: As a parent? You can go back to the argument that women who've had children have not been great writers in our culture. Virginia Woolf, for example, or the Brontës or Jane Austen — these writers were childless. The thought was that children take so much time that, if you were a professional writer, your books would become your babies. In fact, that's often the way it feels to me.

But, of course, one wants to rage against this argument because women are in a unique position — any parent is in a unique position — watching a child grow up. You have this growth of sensibility, this growth of awareness, of language coming, of the episodic nature of life intersecting with the child's life. We have a novel there, quite clearly. I think that having children, against all these other arguments and examples, is a good thing. For me, *the* major part of my life, more than writing, I would say, is having had my children.

On a radio show someone once asked me what was the worst thing that had ever happened to me. You know how they get desperate for questions. And I realized that the worst thing had never happened. The worst thing would be to lose a child through death or separation. That would be the hardest thing to bear.

EW: And so, in a sense, that's what you conjured up for your character: the loss of a child through separation. As the mother of five grown children, four of them daughters, this must have been frightening for you to imagine, to even put yourself in that mode for the purposes of fiction.

CS: Yes. To lose a child and to think that perhaps I was the cause of this, something I did or failed to do caused my child to rebel and separate herself from us. I think that responsibility as a parent is always there.

I like to think of this book on these four little legs: this idea of mothers and children; the idea of writers and readers — I wanted to talk about the writing process; I wanted to talk about goodness; and then I wanted to talk about men and women — this gender issue, which interests me so much and has actually been a part of every book I've written. I think I'm always writing about this.

EW: What did you learn for yourself about goodness in the writing of the novel?

CS: I didn't learn as much as I'd like to, but I've had very interesting discussions with people about it. Someone told me the other day that this is going to be the century where we discover the meaning of consciousness. We don't understand it now. It is the big question. I'd like to think that along with the answer to the question of what consciousness is will come the answer to the question of the nature of goodness. I think they'll come together somehow.

EW: In terms of writing about mothers and daughters and parents and children, you've commented that children are not interested in childhood until later in their lives. Your character Danielle Westerman says something similar: "The trouble with children is they aren't interested in childhood."

You haven't written much about your own childhood. We've

talked about this. But you invent a rich fictional childhood for your character Reta, and especially her gropings towards knowledge and awareness. Is this something you remember from your own childhood?

CS: Yes, that feeling of the helplessness of children. The perplexity of the world — how can everyone understand it? Of course, children are terribly afraid of humiliation, so there are many questions they don't ask adults, and they simply live with these mysteries. For example, when I was a child, I used to wonder why, when I looked sideways, I could see through my nose. This was a big secret, and I didn't tell anyone else because I kept looking at other people who had perfectly ordinary noses, without this odd phenomenon. I thought, I can't possibly ask anyone this question, so I lived with the mystery. I think children do. They simply don't understand quite ordinary events, and no one has the time to explain to them, or even knows what those questions are embedded in and what they consist of.

EW: And you wondered how Jesus' halo stayed in place when he moved?

CS: Yes, that was a great worry to me as a child.

EW: Did you figure it out?

CS: I don't know at what age I would have figured out what a halo was — maybe when I learned a bit about art history. But it seemed to me that it was a great mystery.

EW: Another thing Reta does as a young child is crush flower petals, and her mother upbraids her. Was that something that you were trying to figure out by handling the flower petals?

CS: Yes. What's alive, and what isn't? And what kind of impact can we make on things? All these were great puzzles to me as a child.

EW: Your central character, Reta, is a wife, a mother, a translator, and a writer of fiction herself. Your characters have had various creative occupations before. There's a biographer, a quilt-maker and a designer of mazes. But there's supposed to be this rule about writers not writing about writers, novelists. Why did you want to do it?

CS: I know writers shouldn't write about writers. The world is full of other people who are perfectly interesting and do other things, and I'm always looking for novels where, in fact, that is done. In Richard Ford's novel *Independence Day*, he has his main character selling real estate; I thought that was very well done. I like to think of characters in novels having jobs and actually seeing them working; I don't think they should always be publishers or editors or writers.

But when it came right down to it, I had this novel to write, and I wanted to write about what was terribly interesting to me, and that was writing a novel: how you write a novel, how you *make* a novel. I always think of it as novel-making. And so I wanted this woman to be a novel-maker and to talk about some of the restrictions on novel-making in terms of the time in which you set it. You have to think of who your major characters are going to be. What are their jobs? How old are they? What you're going to name them is very important. You'd think this would all be a wonderful fantasy where you're in charge of the world, but in fact some of this is hard work. And you have to set up where they live, all the details of their various houses or apartments. Do they have a car? Do they have a cat? I just find it so interesting, the idea of building a novel and sometimes letting the novel go in different directions than we find in traditional novels, of letting it go and undermining the novel form a little bit. That's what I was doing here with Reta and her novel. She's writing what we call a "light novel," that is, a novel to take to the beach.

EW: You're reminding me of other things here; for example, when it comes to cars, you get your husband to help you with the various models. And where did you get the names for the characters in this novel? I know you used to sometimes visit graveyards to get good names.

CS: You'd think I'd have a whole bagful of names to draw on. But sometimes I just use the phone book. I had originally called Natalie, one of the daughters in the family, Nancy, and when one of my daughters read the manuscript, she said, "Oh, no one is called Nancy anymore. Could you think of something else?" So I turned her into Natalie. It just takes a stroke of a key to do this now. So, yes, names arrive, and either they work or they don't work. I do like short names though.

EW: And why a translator? Why two languages?

CS: I've always thought that people who have two languages have so much more power than those of us with just one. If you have a foot in another language, in another culture, I think you have a much surer stance in the world, so I wanted her to be a translator.

EW: Is it a Canadian gesture, the French and English?

CS: Of course, yes, it's Canadian to have these two languages.

EW: Reta's emotional journey in this book is reflected in her own process of writing a novel, and sometimes her voice seems to blur with your own. In the first chapter, she says she wants to write a novel "about something happening, about characters moving against a 'there.'" And then she admits, "I have no idea what will happen in this book. I've stumbled up against this idea . . . and now the urge to write won't go away. But it's going to be a book about lost children, about goodness, going home, being happy, and trying to keep the poison of the printed page in perspective." And she says, "I'm desperate to know how the story will turn out." What's that about?

CS: I never know where my novels are going when I sit down and begin them, and I think most novelists would tell you this. I think the direction of the novel comes out of the process of writing, out of what seems more and more to be the inevitable ending to it, and I trust that process to a certain extent now.

On the other hand, there is a way in which every novel is about finding this place we call home. I think all of Jane Austen's novels, for example, are about that: the place where you really belong, the place you've been assigned to but some- how haven't got to. The idea of lost children, adults as lost children, dealing with a script that they hadn't expected to deal with — that's what novels are about. I don't think they're about spectacular good luck or bad luck. I think they're about what happens to us every day. Ordinary everyday life is hard enough, God knows, and presents difficulties for us. Novels are about difficulty.

EW: You say that one of the things that you wanted to do with the novel is turn it around a little bit, play with the form. Is that part of Reta being self-conscious about not knowing how the story will turn out?

CS: Yes. I love the idea of — I don't know why, because I think, in everyday life, I've been quite conventional — of novels that take an unconventional turn, that in fact invert the process of the novel or introduce some huge digression or have a sense of living tissue to them. Novels are enormously expansive, capacious. They'll hold everything. I had this sense years ago, when I was writing *Swann*, that the novel would hold everything I could put into it. I think contemporary novels do this. They pick up that old form and put more in.

EW: Where Reta says she's "trying to keep the poison of the printed page in perspective," apart from its literary value, what's that?

CS: I guess it's literature as life. Literature, instead of life, can get you into some dangerous places, where you only live off the printed page. But I'm very hopeful that the book, as we know it, will survive. I've heard arguments on the other side. But I think that the actual cognitive act of transforming print into meaning is so humanly satisfying that we're going to go on reading books. I can't imagine that we're not going to.

EW: Has it been liberating to enter, as you say, these "incestuous waters"? As your character Reta puts it, "to write about a woman writing"?

CS: Yes, these *are* incestuous waters, to write about a woman writing about a woman writing, yes. I feel that these are all the things a writer shouldn't do, but, just for once, I'm going to allow myself to do it.

EW: You have a paragraph, basically one long sentence, describing what a novel can do. This is where your character Reta is sitting in a garden on a holiday in France, in Burgundy, and thinking about what a novel can do. I hear *your* voice saying what you love about novels.

CS: Yes, I love novels. Novels have been a great consolation.

EW: Reading them? Writing them?

CS: Reading them. I'm reading novels a lot this year, one after another. And, of course, once you read a lot of novels, you want to write one. It's a miraculous form, it seems to me, and it's been so late in coming to us, when you think of all that literature, all that epic poetry we had to put up with.

EW: Like your previous work, this novel *Unless* insists on the importance of the particular as a way of understanding immensity. Reta wants to write about "the overheard and the glimpsed." Her librarian friends share her passion for novels that "describe the unwrittenness of unremarkable men and women." And there's another one, another friend, who's on the lookout for "the arbitrary, the odd, the ordinary, the mucilage of daily life that cements our genuine moments of being." And all of this could apply to you. Was there a need for you in this novel to define, and perhaps defend, your own approach to fiction?

CS: Not defend, but maybe to define. Because it is something I've been thinking about. Why do we read novels? What do they do for us? For me, they allow me into other consciousnesses. I can go where other people think and escape for a minute this voice in my head, the woman who lives in there — her again — and know how this other person thinks. Novels give us access to the thought processes as well as the thoughts of other people, and I think that's a kind of contact that we need and maybe don't have enough of in our regular conversation. We have to have this other layer that connects us more deeply.

I sometimes feel, when I'm reading a book, that the author, the novelist, is speaking straight into my ear. That it's only for me. Of course, it's not. It's for thousands of others. But the intimacy of that novelistic voice can be there, and I suppose that's something that I would like to learn to do.

I like what Susan Sontag said about the novel: that it lets you take an issue or an idea and look at it from all sides, instead of just one side, the way an essayist has to make a premise and defend it, and so on. Novelists aren't restricted to this argument at all. They can quickly change sides, and it gives them a great deal of nimbleness of spirit, I think, and view-taking. I just feel delighted to be a novelist. I have a friend who suggests the novel is really a sphere. We think of it as this rectangular block, but it's really a sphere that we open, and I like this thought very much — that it allows us access to any place.

EW: I always felt that the voice inside *your* head was a more interesting voice than most.

It's curious you have Reta's mentor, Danielle Westerman, as embodying a kind of eighteenth-century sensibility that doesn't like novels, doesn't think they're worthwhile. She says to Reta, "What's really the point of novel-writing when the unjust world howls and writhes?" How would you answer that?

CS: I can't answer it very well, but the point is that the novel keeps us in contact with voices other than our own. I think the worst place to end up is where you're imprisoned in your own voice and your own thoughts, without knowing how other minds work.

EW: Reta has achieved literary success with her first novel, and she plans to write another light novel, a beach book, a charming, romantic comedy called *My Thyme Is Up*. One critic commented that "She was good at happy moments, but inept at the lower end of the keyboard." You have the *New York Times* saying that her book is "very much for the moment, though certainly not for the ages." Much later, that first novel is reassessed and appreciated, and what's simple is now seen as subtle. You've had a bit of that lightweight treatment yourself in response to your earlier so-called "domestic fiction." Do you feel vindicated through Reta?

CS: What I was talking about in this instance was the fact that we have these arbitrary divisions: light fiction, meaningful fiction, heavy fiction, solid fiction, classic fiction. We have all

those classifications. Now, when the novel first landed on us ·
in the eighteenth century, we didn't have any of those. Fiction
was fiction. It was approached differently, of course, and it
was often epistolary in nature, but we didn't have all these
divisions. Now we do, and I think we have to question how we
make these classifications. And are they always just? What do
we award seriousness to? And what does "seriousness" mean?
Naturally, all novelists write the best book they can possibly
write. They write from as deeply into their minds as they can
go. I think we have to rethink some of these classifications of
fiction. That was partly what I was talking about.

EW: And were you getting in a few swipes about your own
treatment in some reviews?

CS: Certainly, my very early novels were treated as domestic
fiction. I'm not quite sure what that means. I wasn't quite sure
even then because we all have a domestic life, and somehow
that life has to appear in our fictions.
    I think I always believed in the serious life of women. I
never doubted that women were to be taken seriously and I
valued women's minds. I think that kept me from believing
those reviews. I felt quite sure of that.

EW: When Reta's talking about the kinds of books that she likes,
she says she's not really interested in poetic novels and postmodern novels or "writers who play games for their own selfish
amusement, who put a chair in every chapter just to be baffling
and obscure." You've put a chair in every chapter. Why?

CS: Oh, because I'm not really Reta, and I like novels that play
games with language, and I like doing this kind of thing. I suppose I do it for the acutely aware reader, but I do it for myself
just out of interest, for my own pleasure. I had this notion of
a seated woman, a kind of woman in repose who is taking in
the world from that position — not a fighting position, not

a standing position, not a sleeping position, but seated and composed — and I just wanted to do it. It was a kind of a game, yes, I confess.

EW: In fact, Reta, near the end of the novel, talks about this almost painterly image of a woman seated. Why that image? It sounds a bit too passive for the sort of feminist fierceness of the book.

CS: Yes, seated can be passive. But it can also be very alert and engaged, and that's how I saw it: a woman seated but aware and listening.

EW: In the opening chapter of *Unless*, Reta describes the ending of a novel. She says a "corruption of cause and effect and the gathering together of all the characters into a framed operatic circle of consolation and ecstasy, just for a moment, just an atomic particle of time." And her own novel-in-progress finds its own surprise ending. She says, "I've bundled up each of the loose narrative strands. For five minutes, a balance has been achieved at the margin of the novel's thin textual plane. Make that five seconds. Make that the millionth part of a nanosecond." Are endings hard for you?

CS: I suppose I don't believe in endings, really. When do you stop a novel, and what do you offer the reader at that point? I have often closed my novels neatly with a number of things brought forward and put together at the last moment. But I've never thought of them as endings, exactly. In other words, there's a life outside the novel; there has been all the way through the novel. There's life outside the novel, in the beginning and in the trajectory of the novel, and the novel goes on afterwards. I've always believed in this *outside*, this great cloud of realness around the novel. So it's just an arbitrary moment, I think, that the novelist chooses to bring things to a conclusion, and it sounds as though every little strand has been put in this tidy knot. But, in fact, we know better. Anyone who lives an ordinary life knows better, because those knots aren't going to stay done for more than two minutes, and they're soon changing shape and asking for more attention. So it's a convention, but it's a convention I rather love.

EW: You talk about the pleasures of reading novels, but how do you feel you've been shaped by your writing, by writing novels?

CS: I suppose the novels have come out of different periods of my life. I recently tried to read my first novel, *Small Ceremonies*, and I couldn't. Now, I wrote that novel in my late thirties, and I thought it might be interesting to see who that woman was, that woman who was trying to write a novel. And I just didn't get very far with it. I kept watching this author strike poses, and there was language that I thought was too pared down, and I didn't feel comfortable with the novel particularly. I don't think it went deep enough.

EW: How have you been affected by the novel *Unless*, in particular?

CS: I've never believed in this idea that novels "write themselves." The character takes over, the plot takes over — they write themselves. I have always raised one eyebrow at that suggestion. I've never believed it. The writer has to do it all. You do the beginning, you do the middle, you do the end — you have to do every bit of it.

But there was in this novel — and I don't know why, I can't explain why — a sense of it almost flying to its conclusion for me. I don't want to get too whimsical about this, but it did feel that there was a kind of inevitability about the way the novel would turn out. I finished it last summer, in three months, in a burst of good health, and it just seemed a wonderful writing time for me.

But I was saying that novels come out of different times in your life, when you're interested in different things. The things I was interested in when I was in my forties are not the same things that I'm interested in now. I think you have to write from where you are.

I used to ask my writing students not to bring manuscripts from the beginning or intermediate creative writing classes to my advanced class. Write from where you are at the moment. Some of them did, and some of them didn't. If we're going to bring any freshness to our writing or any sense of a person behind that print, I think you have to write what you're thinking about right now.

EW: The idea of flying — that sounds wonderful.

CS: It was a wonderful experience. When I finished this book — and I can remember writing "The End" — I felt like I wanted to go out into the street and give people money and do their mending for them or whatever. It felt so good to come to the end of this novel.

EW: You said some time ago that, with age, you get braver about what you can say and what you think can be understood. When Reta expresses her indignation about the powerlessness of women, she says, "I'm willing to blurt it out, if only to myself. Blurting is a form of bravery." I think this is a brave novel. Does it feel that way to you?

CS: It does in a way, yes. I suppose I did some of the things I'd wanted to do in a novel. I wanted, of course, to write about a writer. I wanted to write about a happy marriage. I think that's a kind of departure these days. I wanted to see if I could write a novel about a happy marriage where the underpinning of the marriage wasn't always under assault, as it is in most of the novels we read. I wanted to write about the unsentimental love of children, the strong ties that we don't express. We don't express the idea of these ties very often in words, but you see it everywhere, the intensity between parents and children. I wanted to write about that.

And, of course, I wanted to write about the acceptance of women into literature on their own terms. I don't think this has happened, as I said, and how are we going to make it happen? We're going to have to change what we think of as literature, to a certain extent, in order for women to be fully felt, I think, in our writing. We have wonderful women writers here in Canada, England, the United States, India — everywhere — wonderful women writers who are bringing us their experience. And their work is an oeuvre; it has a different shape to it, and it's not going to fit with the old formula of novels. Women's writing is going to remake our literature and make it whole, I think.

EW: And are you braver?

CS: Yes, I suppose I'm braver because I'm at the end of my life or near the end of my life.

EW: So there's nothing to lose.

CS: I have nothing to lose.

EW: The epigraph for *Unless* is from George Eliot: "If we had a keen vision and feeling of all ordinary human life, it would be like hearing the grass grow and the squirrel's heartbeat, and we should die of that roar which lies on the other side of silence." Why did you choose that?

CS: It's a good question. I don't really believe that you *have* to have an epigraph, and my early books didn't. I thought they were pretentious, especially books that had three epigraphs.

EW: I thought just epigraphs in foreign languages, untranslated, were pretentious.

CS: Oh, yes, that's super pretentious. But I always read them. When I read novels, I always read the epigraphs because I can feel the novelist telling me, This is the way I want to go, so I read them with this idea in mind.

I love *Middlemarch*. I guess I've always believed that much of the world goes on in silence, is never verbalized, is never written down; it's a commonality that we all know and agree upon, and we know we know it. This speaks to that idea.

EW: And, of course, silence does come into play in terms of the daughter's response to her exclusion from the world or what has happened to her. Even Reta's mother-in-law retreats into a kind of silence of invisibility, neglect, with no one bothering to ask her a question. So there are levels of silence.

CS: Yes. I think there are people who wait their whole lifetimes to be asked certain questions, particularly the question "Are you happy?" And it never arrives. My guess is that people are ready to answer those questions, but they don't get asked.

EW: Are you happy?

CS: I'm happy, yes.

EW: You contributed to a recent performance in Toronto called *Mortality*. When you were first invited to write about mortality, did you know what you wanted to say?

CS: No, I didn't. A very nice man I didn't know, Ross Manson, invited me to be part of this. He said there will be some other writers writing about the question of mortality, and I had to tell him that it is not a question that I have addressed in my life. Somehow, I've been too preoccupied. I can only guess that's the reason. I have not spent a lot of time thinking about my death, about the end of life. I suppose I always thought I'd live to be a hundred and go hiking and be one of those great old women who are still baking apple pies at ninety-eight. I didn't get busy and write immediately, and Ross was wondering why I hadn't. In the meantime, I had been diagnosed with a terminal illness, and I started to write out of what my immediate concerns were at that time, a kind of restlessness and inability to find a calm place. So I wrote a first draft that spoke about that: the difficulty of sleeping, of letting go of consciousness, and so on.

The project is now three years old, so I did a revision recently, and I realized that I could speak out of a calm place, that I had arrived there. Three years is a long time to survive, and I've had a chance to think about what my life has meant and what the arc of that life has been like, and to accept the ending of life. When you say, "Are you happy?" yes, I'm happy because I am at peace about this. I've been allowed to write books. I haven't had to be anyone's boss. I never wanted to be anyone's boss. I haven't had anyone bossing me except at the university, and there's not much of that there. I've been able to be independent. I've had wonderful friends. I have seen my children grow up and have children of their own. I've got to the age of sixty-six, which I think now is quite a grand old age.

EW: In *Unless*, you quote John Quincy Adams on his deathbed saying, "I am composed," and your character says, "How admirable and enviable and unbelievable this is."

CS: Yes, I loved this. Famous last lines that people have uttered — we like to collect them. I didn't know if I believed this one: "I am composed." It would certainly be a nice note to go out on, if it is, indeed, a true story.

EW: The character in *Mortality* seems to alternate between struggling against dying and being at peace.

CS: Yes.

EW: And you were saying that you have become less sentimental about death.

CS: Yes. I got less sentimental, more vernacular. You know all
the funny expressions about death, like "hopping the twig" or
"joining the choir invisible."

EW: I've never heard "hopping the twig."

CS: Oh, "hopping the twig" — that was one from my childhood. You think that's all that's going to happen to you. You're
just going to hop the twig.

EW: Perhaps one of the most chilling things that your character
in *Mortality* says is, "Ultimately, the truth, though rarely admit-
ted, is that there is very little that anyone can do for anyone
else."

CS: Yes. I think this is true, in a certain way. People have done
a lot for me. But you come to a point where you have to do
it yourself and construct your own place, and you have to do
it alone.

EW: How have you found the strength to do that?

CS: It's been very gradual. I've found it through talking to
people, through reading novels — I always come back to reading novels — an awareness of how we do this part of our life
by ourselves.

EW: In the end, your character says, "It's a matter of waiting
things out in an improvised shelter and thinking about yourself
as kindly as possible." Are you able to think about yourself
kindly?

CS: Relatively, I think, yes.

EW: Your character Reta says, "I seem to have a knack for self-forgiveness."

CS: Yes. Self-forgiveness helps a lot, I suppose. The feeling that there aren't too many regrets. And I do feel that I don't have too many regrets. But I suppose I regret moments when I've been flippant or overly ironic or careless. I feel I've been awake in the world at a most interesting time, these last fifty years. I think it's been a particularly interesting time as a woman to be awake and aware. I've seen a lot happen. I suppose the next fifty years will be just as full of these rapid changes, but this has been a very full lifetime for me.

EW: Do you ever think in terms of "something, *unless* something," if we go back to that funny word?

CS: Do you mean in terms of something after this life? No, I don't. I never think in terms of something after this life. This is it, and this is why we have to use the time we've got to blurt —

EW: To blurt bravely?

CS: Lots of blurting — blurt bravely and get some words on paper and have lots of conversations with lots of people. I think that's very important — connecting and having conversations, that's a huge part of my life. Being interested. Somehow, I've been able to remain interested in everything that's happening, and you want to hang on to that as long as you can.

EW: As the character in the performance piece *Mortality* says, she goes "right up to the wall." It's not even a breath away.

CS: Yes. I find that a very comforting thought. If you think of death as a part of life — and, in fact, it is — it just intersects exactly with it, and it's just a breath away. It's not that big a thing.

EW: I want to thank you for so many conversations, and particularly for this one.

CS: Thank you, Eleanor.

Acknowledgements

For such a little book my debts are large. First my thanks go to Don Shields for his encouragement with this, and for friendship over the years. Similarly, to Carroll Klein, whose reassuring combination of enthusiasm and expertise made editing these conversations a pleasure. Ian Godfrey aided and abetted the process with the accuracy of his transcribing.

Most of these interviews were first recorded for broadcast on CBC Radio's *Writers & Company*, and I feel very fortunate to enjoy the continuing collaboration of the show's talented and generous producers, Sandra Rabinovitch and Mary Stinson. In two instances here, I also had the opportunity to work with Peter Kavanagh and Ann Jansen. The thoughtfulness and good humour of associate producer Nancy McIlveen is an enormous boon, as is the camaraderie of executive producer Susan Feldman.

Above all, thanks to listeners, whose responses make my work an unfailing source of satisfaction and reward. Carol Shields talks about the intimacy of the novelist's voice speaking straight into her ear. What a privilege for me to have access to that kind of experience through the medium of radio.

For this book, the energy of Susanne Alexander and everyone at Goose Lane Editions, as well as my agent, Jackie Kaiser, was indispensable.

I was invited by Karen Konstantynowicz of *Room of One's Own* to contribute the essay that became "Scrapbook of Carol." I would like to thank Monica Penner and Ana Torres, the issue's editors.

As always, I am most grateful for the constancy, affection and support of family and friends. In particular, Marta Braun's curiosity, counsel and emergency editing are invaluable. A special thanks to the Landfall Trust in Brigus, Newfoundland. To Gayla Reid for the perpetual pursuit of puffins (and all that entails). And to Sherry Simon for insisting that I write.

Award-winning writer and broadcaster Eleanor Wachtel is widely regarded as one of Canada's best interviewers. She is the host of CBC Radio's *Writers & Company* and *Wachtel on the Arts*.

Wachtel was born in Montreal, where she studied English literature at McGill University. She later lived in the United States and Kenya, and in the mid-1970s, she worked as a freelance writer and broadcaster in Vancouver.

In the fall of 1987, she moved to Toronto to work as a literary commentator on CBC Radio's *State of the Arts*. She has hosted *Writers & Company* since its inception in 1990. She also hosted *The Arts Tonight* from 1996 until 2007. Both programs won CBC Radio Awards for Excellence. In one instance, the judges noted that if they had to take one hour of radio to a desert island, it would be *Writers & Company*.

Eleanor Wachtel has published three books of interviews: *Writers & Company*, *More Writers & Company*, and *Original Minds*. She is a contributor to the bestseller *Dropped Threads*, edited by Carol Shields and Marjory Anderson, and *Lost Classics*, edited by Michael Ondaatje et al. Wachtel is the winner of the Jack Award for the promotion of Canadian books, as well as the recipient of six honorary degrees. In 2005, she became a Member of the Order of Canada.